C000220444

EARLY RAILWAYS OF MANCHESTER

ANTHONY DAWSON

AMBERLEY

First published 2017

Amberley Publishing
The Hill, Stroud,
Gloucestershire, GL5 4EP

www.amberley-books.com

ISBN: 978 1 4456 6518 4 (print)
ISBN: 978 1 4456 6519 1 (ebook)

British Library Cataloguing in Publication Data.
A catalogue record for this book is available from the British Library.

Typeset in 10pt on 13pt Celeste.
Typesetting by Amberley Publishing.
Printed in the UK.

Contents

	Acknowledgements	5
Chapter 1	Manchester, the Railway City	6
Chapter 2	The Manchester, Bolton & Bury Railway (1838)	21
Chapter 3	The Manchester & Leeds Railway (1840)	41
Chapter 4	The Manchester & Birmingham Railway (1842)	70
Conclusion	Consolidation and Amalgamation	89
	Select Bibliography	95

Acknowledgements

I should like to thank all those who have helped this book come to fruition: Andy Mason for his patient support of my literary efforts and for his maps; Lauren Jaye Gradwell for the use of photographs; the Museum of Science & Industry, Manchester; and my fellow MOSI Railway Volunteers.

Abbreviations

GJR	Grand Junction Railway
GWR	Great Western Railway
L&B	London & Birmingham Railway
L&M	Liverpool & Manchester Railway
LNWR	London & North Western Railway
LYR	Lancashire & Yorkshire Railway
M&B	Manchester & Birmingham Railway
M&L	Manchester & Leeds Railway
MB&B	Manchester, Bolton & Bury Railway
MS&L	Manchester, Sheffield & Lincolnshire Railway
MSJ&A	Manchester, South Junction & Altrincham Railway
SA&M	Sheffield, Ashton-under-Lyne & Manchester Railway

CHAPTER 1

Manchester, the Railway City

Even before it was opened, the perceived automatic success of the Liverpool & Manchester Railway led to a flurry of railway schemes, not just linking Manchester to neighbouring towns, but as far afield as Chester. In November 1830 alone – two months after the L&M opened – railways from Manchester to Leeds, Sheffield, from Preston to Wigan, Oldham to Manchester, and even Liverpool to Leeds and London to Birmingham were proposed. Manchester and Liverpool found themselves at the heart of this new railway boom. Manchester rapidly became not only the world's first industrial city, but also the world's first railway city; within a decade, it was joined by an iron road to Leeds, Sheffield, Birmingham, and London.

MANCHESTER RAILWAYS C.1855

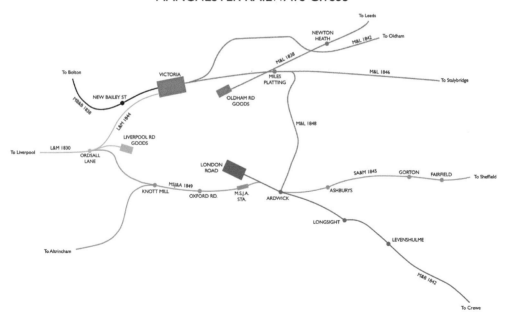

Map of Manchester's railways c. 1855. (Andy Mason)

Manchester in the 1830s

Manchester was Britain's first industrial city, with its economy based on the cotton trade; the first cotton mill, built by Richard Arkwright, was opened in 1781 on Shudehill (the subject of a dig by Channel 4's *Time Team* in 2005) and by 1816 there were eighty-six steam-powered cotton spinning factories. The massive expansion in the cotton trade in Manchester had first been fuelled by the 'first transport revolution' of the canals, making Manchester a Georgian boom town; but it was with the coming of the railways that Manchester developed into 'Cottonopolis'. The rapid rise in factory-based industrialisation led to an equally rapid rise in population, doubling in twenty years from 75,281 to 126,066 in 1821. Living conditions in the industrial city for the mill workers was appalling – the Manchester Statistical Society reported in 1833 that there were 37,000 worker's dwellings, of which 10,000 were 'unsuitable' slum dwellings, and that 18,000 people lived in cellars. Friedrich Engels described these horrendous living conditions; 'A whole family is often accommodated in a single bed … often more than one family lived in a damp cellar, containing only one room, in whose pestilential atmosphere, dwelled sixteen persons.'

The number of cotton mills in Manchester reached its zenith in 1850; there were 172 textile mills and 91 textile-finishing sites within the city limits. Other industries grew up to support the textile trade, notably engineering and the building trade, to construct the mills and supply them with cotton machinery and steam engines. Manchester led the way in iron founding and casting with the likes of William Fairbairn and Eaton Hodgkinson. Firms such as David Bellhouse & Sons – builders, engineers, and iron-founders – specialised in iron-framed fireproof mill buildings.

Despite its industrial might, Manchester remained 'the greatest mere village in England'. Prior to the Municipal Corporations Act of 1835 Manchester was governed, as in the medieval period, by the Parish Vestry Meeting, which was naturally restricted to members of the Church of England, leaving non-conformists (who by 1820 outnumbered the Anglicans) disenfranchised. Thus, it is not surprising that the campaign for incorporation was led by prominent Unitarians, father and son Thomas (the first Mayor of Manchester) and John Potter, and the Quaker Richard Cobden. Although the Charter was granted in 1838, legal objections were raised – not least from the ancient Lords of the Manor, the Mosleys – so the leading members of Cross Street Chapel lent money to 'tide over the situation'. The Charter was granted a year later but it was not until 1843 that the new council was able to 'enter fully upon the enjoyment of the privileges' granted to it. Finally, in 1846, the Council purchased the Manor of Manchester from Sir Oswald Mosley for £200,000.

Society in Manchester was divided on political and religious grounds: Anglican Tory versus Liberal Nonconformist and Radical Dissenters. It was also a period of great social upheaval globally, with revolution in France toppling the Bourbon Monarchy, and Liberal uprisings in Poland, Hungary, and Italy. At home there were all the political machinations surrounding Chartism, the repeal of the Corn Laws, and the passing of the Reform Act (1832). Denied any civil rights until the repeal of the Test Act (which restricted public office and certain careers solely to Anglicans) in 1828, Dissenters put their energies for self-improvement into the world of business. The lack of dogma, and their belief in 'Freedom, Reason, and Tolerance', combined with their intellectual curiosity, led them to reject traditional modes of thought and into emerging areas of business and trade, which had not yet been 'professionalised' into institutions with their concomitant links with the establishment (Crown and Church). This interest in new ideas gelled perfectly with the status of Dissenters as 'outsiders'; as open-minded freethinkers.

It is not surprising, therefore, that Manchester's business and social élite was centred on the Unitarian chapels on Mosley Street and Cross Street. At Mosley Street, membership included the industrialists Thomas, John, and Edmund Potter, Robert Hyde Greg (owner of Quarry Bank Mill), the engineer Peter Ewart (he was employed by Greg as Engineer from the 1790s), the Murrays, John Kennedy, and James McConnell. John Kennedy was a judge at the Rainhill Trials, and his brother, James, joined with Edward Bury to be the 'brains' behind Bury, Curtis & Kennedy; locomotive manufacturers of Liverpool. Cross Street numbered William Fairbairn and Eaton Hodgkinson as members during the fifty-six-year Ministry of Reverend William Gaskell, who was perhaps one of the most important Unitarians nationally. His wife, of course, was the author Elizabeth Gaskell. Revd William was president of the 'Portico Library' and also a member of the 'Manchester Literary and Philosophical Society', the leading institution in the town. We will meet other members of

Cross Street Chapel: the powerhouse of nineteenth-century Manchester. Sadly, this building (dating to 1694) was destroyed by enemy action in December 1940. Happily the congregation thrives in a more modern building. (Author's Collection)

his congregation later, including John and Ann Hawkshaw – Ann was a noted poet – Henry Houldsworth – a wealthy cotton spinner – and the solicitor Samuel Dukinfield Darbishire. Edward Watkin (the son of the prosperous Unitarian cotton merchant Absalom Watkin) the general manager of the Sheffield, Ashton-under-Lyne & Manchester Railway was also a congregant. Under his vision the 'Great Central Mainline' was built. Watkin later converted to Anglicanism as it was 'more respectable' than the religion of his birth and opened far more 'establishment' doors. His brother, Alfred, became Mayor of Manchester.

Most of the above were members of the 'Manchester Lit & Phil.' Whilst not restricted solely to Unitarians, members of the 'Lit & Phil.' invariably were, including Robert Owen (of New Lanark), David Bellhouse the builder, and James Watt Jnr (also a member at the Cross Street Unitarian Chapel), as well as Richard Roberts, John Hawkshaw, and John Dalton, the Quaker chemist (a notable exception). Unitarians also came to dominate Manchester politics through the 'Manchester Little Circle'. Of these eleven influential liberal/radical businessmen, seven were Unitarians – five being members of Cross Street. They met in the premises of Unitarian businessman John Potter to organise social and political reform, including repeal of the Corn Laws, extolling the virtues of Free Trade, the likes of the Ten Hour Act, and municipal and governmental reform including: repeal of the Corn Laws; the Ten Hour Act; Governmental and Municipal Reform including extension of the Franchise, getting Manchester its own MP and abolition of Rotten Boroughs. Members of this group also established the Manchester Chamber of Commerce (1824) and the Unitarian-owned and edited *Manchester Guardian* (1821). An offshoot of the 'Lit. & Phil.' was the Manchester Mechanics' Institute.

Revd William Gaskell (1805–1884), Minister at Cross Street for over fifty years, 1828–1884. (Author/Cross Street Chapel)

Their wealth and education – via the Dissenting Academies as Unitarians and other non-Anglicans were barred from the ancient Universities until 1854 – made the Unitarians in particular 'the élite of dissent, and of provincial commercial and industrial life'. Unitarianism, a minority religious belief, was illegal prior to 1813, and it is therefore not surprising that the powerful Unitarians of Manchester and their allies in Liverpool (and elsewhere) favoured their co-religionists with regards to business contracts – such as the two Stephensons, Fairbairn, and Charles Tayleur – leading to complaints of corruption and patronage; a claim easily levelled at the Liverpool & Manchester Railway by their opponents as the two founders, Joseph Sanders and John Kennedy, were Unitarians, as was the secretary and treasurer Henry Booth and the chief engineer, George Stephenson. The Unitarians and Quakers, although tiny in numbers, wielded a disproportionate level of power and influence in Leeds, Liverpool, Manchester, and Birmingham. Corporately, the Manchester Unitarians – Fieldens, Ashtons, McConnells, Kennedys, Gregs, Houldsworths, and Potters – formed a powerful and extremely wealthy industrial élite, dominating the industrial North West.

These up-and-coming Manchester men were to effectively challenge the older generation of railway promoters, the powerful 'Liverpool Party'. Usually a generation older than the Manchester men, the 'Liverpool Party' had made their wealth from banking, shipping and slavery: John Moss, one of Liverpool's leading businessmen and bankers, and first Chairman of the Liverpool & Manchester, was a well-known slave-owner and as Robert Gwynne of the NRM has suggested, much of the capital for railway schemes in the mid-1830s came from slavery compensation payments following the Slavery Abolition Act of 1836, which made slavery illegal across the British Empire. These were hard-headed businessmen who, in the first half of the nineteenth century, saw the railways as a solid investment. They had also learned many lessons from the Liverpool & Manchester project in the planning and management of the railways. The one goal of the 'Liverpool Party' was to control Britain's burgeoning railway network and as a group they owned majority shareholdings in the London & Birmingham, Grand Junction, Leicester & Swannington, the Eastern Counties and even the Paris & Lyon railways. The 'Liverpool Party' were ardent supporters of the Stephenson *méthode*, with the only opposition coming from the Great Western Railway and Brunel. The 'struggle for the Broad Gauge' was in fact a battle between the 'Liverpool Party' and their opponents. But, by the 1840s, with the second 'Railway Mania' (and its ultimate collapse), the power was shifting away from the 'Liverpool Party' to the up-and-coming second generation of self-made, largely Nonconformist, businessmen. Tiny in comparison, the Manchester & Birmingham Railway and its struggle for existence (*Chapter 4*) was part of this opposition to the 'Liverpool Party'.

Manchester's First Locomotive

The Liverpool & Manchester Railway (L&M) created demand for an entirely new machine – the railway locomotive – and thus it was natural that many Manchester engineering firms contemplated entering what promised to be a lucrative market. Indeed, the L&M were keen to encourage engineers to tender their own designs, to further improvements to the locomotive. In May 1831 the directors advertised tenders for the supply of two locomotives 'equal or superior to the best at present in use on ... the Line'. The aim of the directors – in the spirit of the Rainhill Trials – was to 'obtain the most improved Locomotive Engine that mechanical skill and experience can furnish'. In response, offers came from Sharp, Roberts & Co. and William Fairbairn of Manchester, as well as Edward Bury and George Forrester of Liverpool. Messrs. Galloway, Bowman & Glasgow of the Caledonian Foundry, Bridgwater Street, Manchester, also used this as an opportunity to construct their first locomotive, which John Galloway claimed was 'the first made in Manchester'. Galloway, Bowman & Glasgow had been formed by William Galloway – a Scot – and James Bowman in 1806, with premises on Bridgwater Street, as founders, engineers, and mill-wrights. William Glasgow joined the concern in 1820 from Messrs. Rothwell & Hick of Bolton as junior partner. Galloway & Bowman formed a separate partnership as machine makers *c.* 1828. It is not surprising, therefore, that they were lured into what promised to be a remunerative market for steam locomotives, probably at the suggestion of John Galloway who 'in particular was very interested in the possibilities of the railway locomotive'.

Galloway & Bowman's *Manchester* was completed by the summer of 1831 and underwent trials during August. The *Manchester Times* (3 September 1831), thought it of 'peculiar construction':

> The machinery is *all in sight* – not stowed away under the boiler, but close to the eye and hand of the engineer. Another is that the engineer's station is at the *front* of the engine, so that no obstruction on the road can escape his notice.

Manchester had a pair of vertical cylinders at the front of the locomotive, which measured 11 ½ inches by 16 inches and were placed 'directly over the crank axle, which has wheels of 5 feet 3 inches diameter'. Vertical cylinders were preferred, as it was believed they suffered from less wear than horizontal. The wheels were wooden,

LIVERPOOL AND MANCHESTER RAILWAY—LOCOMOTIVE "MANCHESTER," 1832

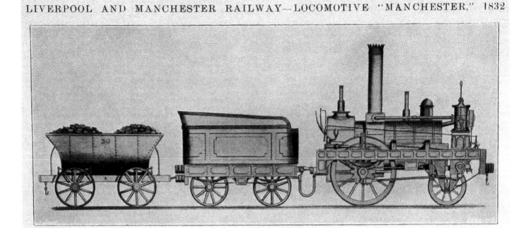

Galloway's unsuccessful locomotive *Manchester* – 'the first built in Manchester'. (Author's collection)

Made by John Ashbury himself, a young man just out of his time, who afterwards founded the great wagon works at Openshaw bearing his name – on to these we shrunk iron welded tyres.

According to John Galloway, there was considerable difficulty in getting *Manchester* from the works to Liverpool Road Station:

We could not put steam on, nor was there a wagon which would take it, so we had to "bar" it down to Ordsal Lane, which took a gang of men with crowbars from 6 p.m. to 9 a.m. The road was not paved with setts as now, but very poorly and irregularly. The news got about that it was going to be tried, and a lot of friends gathered round to take part...

Manchester underwent trials during the last week of August. The *Manchester Courier* reported:

On Monday last, a trial was made on the railway by a new locomotive engine by our townsmen, Galloway, Bowman and Glasgow. The engine had attached to it, besides carriages containing about eighty passengers, a train with goods weighing forty tons. With this heavy load the distance to Newton, fifteen miles, was done in easily in fifty-eight minutes. Here some delay took place from the loss a small bolt, and some further delay took place at the inclined plane till it was cleared of the *Goliath* which had been taking up its load twice. It was supposed by persons on the railway that the new engine would have to do the same thing, but it was determined to try it with the full load. The first half of the rise was gone over at the rate of seven or eight miles an hour, which gradually diminished till it fell to four or five. The engine was thus put to the severest trial and stood it creditably.

Despite having shown *Manchester* to be more than capable, on the return journey from Liverpool 'Mr Glasgow, perhaps grudging to see even an engine with too little to do', ordered that the load be increased:

A train of carriages that stood at the road side loaded with some thirty tons of oak timber were ... attached. This operation occupied about twenty minutes, and then the engine with its great load, came beautifully into Manchester, having exactly occupied two hours on the journey, or one hour and forty exclusive of the stop.

John Galloway left his own vivid impression of another run with *Manchester*:

I got up to half a dozen third-class carriages to run up to Chat Moss and back ... We started off about noon, about 200 in number, and pulled up at the Chat Moss Tavern – this was usual in those days ... We pulled up at Parkside, where we unhooked the wagons, the occupiers of which had quite a holiday in the country ... We turned back on the same line ... A train from Liverpool on its own line was coming up and we ran alongside it for some distance, when, without expecting it, we ran against the points. One wheel remained on the line but the other ran off, straining the crank axle. The engine was quickly pulled up ... It took us an hour or two to get back to Parkside, as the crank axle being crooked, the engine "wobbled" very much.

At Parkside 'Old Fyfe', the Locomotive Superintendent, was despatched to Manchester, and 'he brought another train back to take the party', some of who had decided to walk home which, given the time of year, was not 'disagreeable'. *Manchester* remained at Parkside overnight, and returned to Manchester the following morning by 'taking out the bent axle'.

The L&M did not consent to purchase the *Manchester*, but did allow Messrs. Galloway to hire her to the Haydock Colliery to work their coal trains. *Manchester* was involved in a fatal accident on 2 March 1833 when working an L&M goods train down the Sutton Incline:

> The break became unmanageable. The consequence was that the engine acquired an impetus which threw it off the rails. The engineer, named McCannis, was knocked off the tender onto the road, and the wheels of the train went over his legs ... but he was so much injured before he could be carried to the [Liverpool] infirmary. Another man was slightly maimed in the same accident, but he is expected to recover in a few days.
>
> (*Liverpool Advertiser* 7 March 1833)

The coroner's inquest revealed that *Manchester* was unstable at high speed because of its high centre of gravity and from the effect of the action of the vertical cylinders. The brakes were also considered to be inefficient.

Manchester was subsequently hired to Richard Badnall Esq. for his experiments on the 'undulating railway', in which he believed time lost ascending an incline could be made up for with faster running down the other side. In other words, the antithesis of the Stephenson school, which argued for the flattest gradients possible. Badnall reported that *Manchester* was

> Capable of dragging a considerable load, she was, from her particular construction, by no means adapted to the safe attainment of ... [high] ... velocity ... Mr G Stephenson was in agreement ... her power was not only ineffectual, but she was almost an encumbrance.

Galloway's second engine was far more conventional, but retained vertical cylinders, driving a crankshaft and flycranks between a pair of 5-foot driving wheels. Named *Caledonian*, she was delivered in early autumn 1832. In order to keep the centre of gravity low, she was fitted with an oval boiler. The *Manchester Courier* (29 September 1832) reported:

> On Thursday week, a locomotive engine of entirely new construction, the invention of Messrs. Bowman, Galloway, and Glasgow, of this town, performed an experimental trip upon the railway with a train of loaded wagons. The engine proceeded at a rapid rate from Manchester to Liverpool, and shortly afterwards returned to Manchester. We understand the experiment was highly satisfactory. Unlike the engines of Mr. Stevenson, the cylinders are perpendicular, and are placed on top of the engine.

Galloway's second attempt, *Caledonian*. Later rebuilt and accepted into service on the Liverpool & Manchester. (Author's Collection)

John Galloway's notebooks reveal that on the outward leg, *Caledonian* drew a load of twenty-five wagons from Manchester to Liverpool, departing at 5:30 a.m.; she reached Parkside an hour later and Liverpool at 8:08 a.m. after having 'stopped 8 min. in consequence of losing a cotter' and a further fifteen or so minutes on the Whiston and Sutton inclines. Her tender had been loaded with 1,134 lbs of coke, of which 630 lbs were burned on the journey. A second trip was arranged a week later on 27 September. The L&M purchased *Caledonian* and a spare set of wheels for £800 on 29 October 1832, and was numbered 28 in the L&M fleet. She was sold five years later to the London & Birmingham Railway for £400.

Sharp, Roberts & Co.

Manchester's third locomotive was built by Sharp, Roberts & Co., which had been founded by Richard Roberts, who arrived in Manchester as a penniless Welshman fleeing from the Militia Ballot around 1806; establishing his own firm of tool makers, and supplying parts for textile machinery in 1816. In 1826, Roberts entered into partnership with Thomas Sharp and Robert Chapman Sharp to form Sharp, Roberts & Co. with an international reputation (the firm supplied mill machinery to French companies) for the quality of their cotton mill machinery. Atlas Works was established on Great Bridgewater Street. The firm's first locomotive was built in response to the L&M director's advertisement in May 1831 but, 'at their own request', only tendered to build a single locomotive. Sharp, Roberts & Co. were given the same specification as issued to Bury in Liverpool (15 August 1831) and they offered to the L&M an engine with outside vertical cylinders. The locomotive took over a year to build – Sharp, Roberts reporting in May 1833 that it had been 'working well for a week now'. Named *Experiment*, the locomotive had a pair of vertical cylinders driving through bell-cranks to the connecting rods, and became the prototype for three locomotives supplied to the Dublin & Kingstown Railway in 1834. From experience gained with the vertical-cylindered *Manchester*, the L&M rejected the locomotive; pressed by Sharp, Roberts they offered £800 if they would convert the locomotive to horizontal cylinders with 'spring pistons' and more efficient valves.

Eventually, in February 1834, Sharp, Roberts sold *Experiment* to the L&M for £700, who fitted the new cylinders and valve gear themselves and took it into their stock as number 32. Roberts designed a very successful series of 2-2-2 inside cylinder tender locomotives, which were used by the likes of the Manchester & Birmingham, Sheffield, Ashton-under-Lyne & Manchester, London, Southwestern (for whom they also supplied an 0-4-2 type based on Stephenson & Co.'s 'Large Samson') and the Great Northern Railway. They were soon nicknamed 'Sharpies'. Not content with railway locomotives, Roberts built a 'locomotive carriage, intended for common roads', which was run experimentally along Oxford Road, Manchester, 27 March 1834 carrying some sixty passengers and attaining a maximum speed of 20 mph, but the experiment was cut short for 'want of water'.

In the same year that *Experiment* was sold, the twenty-one-year-old Carl Beyer – a Saxon engineer with little English – joined the firm as a draughtsman, eventually becoming the firm's chief engineer in 1843. Beyer left in 1853 to establish, with Richard Peacock

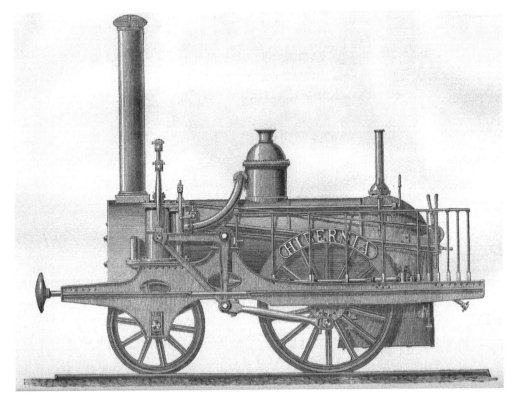

Sharp, Roberts & Co's *Hibernia*, built for the Dublin & Kingstown Railway: *Experiment* was broadly similar. (Author's Collection)

John Sharp, photographed
c. 1850. (Author's Collection)

Charles Patrick Stewart, *c.* 1850.
(Author's Collection)

and Charles Geach, Beyer, Peacock & Co. of Gorton, Manchester. Beyer and Peacock were founder members of the Institution of Mechanical Engineers in 1847.

The partnership of Sharp, Roberts & Co. was dissolved in 1843 when Roberts left, the concern becoming Sharp Brothers & Co. In 1852 Charles Patrick Stewart became a partner upon the retirement of John Sharp, the firm then becoming Sharp, Stewart & Co. of Atlas Works, Manchester. Thomas Sharp retired in the same year and was succeed by Stephen Robinson. As Sharp, Stewart & Co, they obtained the sole rights to the Giffard Injector.

William Fairbairn

Fairbairn was a Scot, who had met and befriended George Stephenson in 1803 whilst the two were apprentices. He moved to Manchester c. 1813 and started his own business in 1817 in partnership with James Lillie, producing mill machinery. Fairbairn and Lillie did not necessarily see eye-to-eye, Lillie admonishing Fairbairn for attending Cross Street Chapel. During the 1820s Fairbairn worked with two other Manchester engineers, Eaton Hodgkinson and Peter Ewart, and together they developed the 'Hodgkinson beam'. It is also interesting to note all three were well-connected Unitarians, Fairbairn and Hodgkinson

Sir William Fairbairn, 1st Baronet of Ardwick (1789–1874): progenitor of the 'Lancashire Boiler', and the Manchester Steam Users Association which still remains as a national certification authority. (Author's Collection)

also being members of the Manchester 'Lit. and Phil.' Another member of Fairbairn's close circle was James Nasmyth of steam-hammer fame. Fairbairn, together with several other leading Unitarian businessmen (George William Wood, Joseph Brotherton, Benjamin Heywood and George Philips) and Richard Roberts, was instrumental in founding the Manchester Mechanics' Institution in 1824, of which Revd William Gaskell was a major

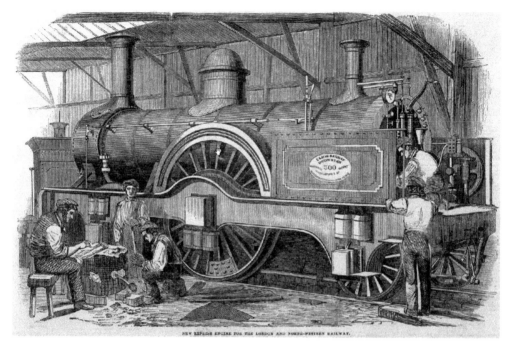

'Locomotive Building' as depicted by the *Illustrated London News* at the Manchester works of William Fairbairn & Son. One of McConnell's Bloomer class is being constructed. (Author's Collection)

A beautiful locomotive for a beautiful lady: *Eugénie*, named after the Empress Eugénie de Montijo of France in 1855. Displayed at the Exhibition Universelle and later taken into the stock of the *Chemin du Fer du Nord* as Machine 164. (Author's Collection)

supporter and early lecturer. Fairbairn and Hodgkinson were later consultants to Robert Stephenson during the construction of his famous tubular bridges at Conwy and the Menai Straits. Due to a recession in the cotton industry in the mid-1830s, the firm diversified into the manufacture of steam engines and iron paddle-steamers.

By 1830, Fairbairn & Lillie had capital of around £40,000 and were employing 300 men. James Lillie left the concern in 1839, which then became William Fairbairn & Sons. They built their first steam locomotives for the Manchester & Leeds Railway in the same year, to a design of Edward Bury of Liverpool. In total the firm supplied sixty-nine locomotives to the M&L. Fairbairn was created a Baronet in 1869, and was also a member of the *Légion d'Honneur* (1855), the same year he exhibited his model locomotive named *Eugénie* – in honour of the Empress of France – at the Exposition Universelle held that year in Paris.

Wagons and Coaches

The railways not only needed locomotives, but also rolling stock. The earliest rolling stock for the Liverpool & Manchester had been built by the father and son team of Thomas Clarke and Nathaniel Worsdell in Liverpool; Thomas resigned from the L&M in January 1837 and in the same year Nathaniel left to become carriage and wagon superintendent of the Grand Junction Railway. They were succeeded by John Pownall on the L&M. In the following year, Nathaniel was engaged as the 'inspector of carriages' on the Manchester & Leeds Railway and employed in a consultative capacity, designing the first carriages for the M&L. Later in the year, Nathaniel recommended his father (Thomas) being appointed as 'inspector of the carriage department' in his stead; he was appointed in February 1839 with a salary of £250 and £50 for his son, who would be retained as a consultant.

One of the first independent firms to meet the demand for railway rolling stock was that of Richard Melling – son of John Melling of the L&M – of Coupland Street, Manchester, who started in business in the early 1830s as coach builders who naturally diversified into railways. In 1838 they advertised:

> On Sale, ready for immediate use. Twenty-two, excellent, well-made, and completely fitted, SECOND CLASS RAILWAY CARRIAGES, nearly similar to those used on the Grand Junction Railway: may be had on very reasonable terms.

Their first major order was for six first-class coaches for the L&M in 1836, for delivery by summer 1837, as the L&M carriage shops could not meet demand. In December 1839 Melling & Co. received an order for second-class carriages for the Manchester & Leeds, at £150 each. Mellings were also asked to convert ten second-class carriages into firsts for £39 each. Melling designed some unusual rolling stock for the M&L; both 18 feet long and 7 feet wide, it was built 'after the fashion of a gondola', with a central compartment 7 feet long, 'fitted up with splendid mahogany sofas lined with crimson plush and trimmed with silk...', and with plate glass windows and curtains. The two open ends were fitted with waterproof hoods. They were painted yellow with the arms of Manchester, Leeds, Bradford, York, Hull, and Sheffield on the door panels. It was also probably Melling who designed a composite first- and second-class carriage for the M&L, consisting of three compartments – two open at either end (second-class) with a fully enclosed first-class compartment in the centre.

Melling & Co. supplied first-class coaches to the Sheffield, Ashton-under-Lyne & Manchester Railway in 1845, on condition that the builders kept them in good repair for a period of twelve months. Mellings also supplied the SA&M with double-decked sheep wagons – presumably based on their earlier designs for the L&M – in 1843.

Perhaps the most famous firm was that of John Ashbury, who established the Ashbury Railway Carriage & Iron Co. in 1837 at Knott Mill, in the Castlefield area of Manchester; close to the Liverpool Road terminus of the L&M. The firm moved to Openshaw in 1841 where they produced railway carriages, wheels, and axles. The works occupied about 20 acres and at its height employed 2,000 staff.

CHAPTER 2

The Manchester, Bolton & Bury Railway (1838)

Amongst the earliest of the various Manchester railway schemes was the Manchester, Bolton & Bury Railway, which took its name from its progenitor – the Manchester, Bolton & Bury Canal & Navigation Co. The canal company had been incorporated by an Act of 13 May 1791, to build a canal between those three towns. The first section of

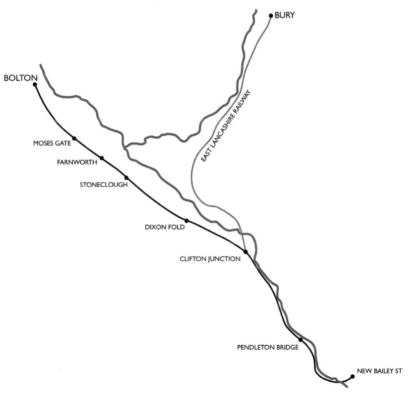

The Manchester, Bolton & Bury Railway and its allied canal. (Andy Mason)

the canal opened in 1796 and was open throughout by 1798. It was never a profitable concern, accruing a staggering amount of debt necessitating additional Acts to give the company power to raise extra capital to complete the undertaking. Success of the nearby Bolton & Leigh Railway (opened in 1828) and the Liverpool & Manchester (1830) led to the formation of a committee of Bolton gentlemen to consider the possibility of a more direct railway between Bolton and Manchester, rather than the B&L, which met the L&M at Kenyon Junction 13 miles west of Manchester. The *Bolton Chronicle* (31 July 1830) describes a meeting in Bolton of the subscribers to the new railway; already some £66,700 had been subscribed and it was proposed to appoint John M. Rastrick – engineer of the Huddersfield Canal – as Engineer. The provisional committee of the railway felt able to issue a *Prospectus* in August. A General Meeting of the MB&B was held on 10 September 1830, at the Bridge Inn, Bolton, to discuss the drawings and plans prepared by Rastrick, 'and to decide upon the line to be adopted'.

At the same time as moves were afoot to build the railway from Bolton to Manchester, a separate scheme for a line from Bolton to Preston was also inaugurated. At a joint meeting on 13 November 1830 at the Bridge Inn, Bolton, the two concerns decided to 'consolidate ... into one; so that there will now be a direct line from Manchester to Preston, through Bolton, and Chorley, with branches to Bury, Blackburn, and Wigan'. The Bolton and Preston railway was to be revived in 1836 and incorporated in March 1837.

A new survey was made by John Urpeth Rastrick, and his intent was to fill in the canal, lay the railway line on top, and to use a cable-worked incline plane over the summit at Prestolee. The Act for conversion of the canal to a railway was granted 23 August 1831; a second Act was obtained in 1832, which granted the company the right to lay the railway *alongside* the canal and allowing it to raise £46,000 through shares and loans. A third Act of 17 June 1835 finalised the route of the railway and authorised the formation of a joint stock company and a fourth Act, 11 June 1838, allowed the company to raise further capital through loans.

As with the L&M, most of the money for the MB&B came from Liverpool; the directors included wealthy Liverpool merchants and bankers such as James Brancker (the Chairman); John Bibby (a ship owner who was murdered in 1840); and members of the powerful Dissenting family, the Rathbones – William Rathbone was also a shareholder of the L&M whilst Theodore Woolman Rathbone was Chairman of the Bolton & Leigh Railway and a Director of the Manchester, Bury & Rossendale Railway. James Ritson was the treasurer and Samuel Dukinfield Darbishire was their solicitor.

The first engineer was one Alexander Nimmo, but he died in 1831 and was replaced by Jesse Hartley. Hartley was a Yorkshire Dissenter, born in Pontefract in 1780, and was also Civil Engineer and Surveyor to the Mersey Dock & Harbour Board, and who rebuilt the Liverpool Docks between 1831 and 1859. He was succeeded as engineer by another Yorkshire Dissenter, John – later Sir John – Hawkshaw, who came to the post of Engineer and Manager at the youthful age of only twenty-one, and would be retained by the Lancashire & Yorkshire Railway. Hartley's final costing was £254,755. Construction started under the guidance of Hartley in 1833 and in June 1835 he reported that the railway would be open by spring 1837. The line appears to have been built with little trouble; the only major engineering feats being the 295-yard-long Farnworth Tunnel and the cutting at Pepper Hill, Clifton, which was 101 feet deep. For most of its route the railway followed

Jesse Hartley's magnificent bridge over Stoneclough Road at Kearsley on the Manchester, Bolton & Bury Railway. (Author)

that of the canal and was carried on extensive embankments, and at Clifton a retaining wall was built to support the railway embankment as it ran alongside the canal embankment. The branch to Bury was authorised in the Acts of 1831–1835 but never built. Bury would be linked to the MB&B at Clifton (which became Clifton Junction) in 1846 with the opening of the Manchester, Bury & Rossendale Railway, which formed part of the East Lancashire Railway.

Opening the Line

Compared to its larger neighbour, the L&M, the MB&B had been comparatively cheap: £526,235 6s 5d. The first train from Manchester to Bolton left New Bailey Street station on 17 May 1838, conveying the company's directors and their invited guests; probably totalling around 150 all told. The *Preston Chronicle* (2 June 1838) reported that

> At eleven o'clock, the directors ... started from the station, New Bailey-street, Salford by a first-class train. The day was beautiful, and as the train glided through the valley of the Irk, the rapidly changing scenery seemed like the sudden changes of a panorama. The distance to Agecroft station was completed in seven minutes. From that spot to within about a mile of Bolton the close succession of romantic and picturesque scenery along the line will bear comparison with the view from any railway in the Kingdom.

The *Kendal Mercury*, however, noted that

> The time fixed for the departure of the trains was eleven o'clock; but the first train moved off from the station at New Bailey-street exactly at two-minutes before eleven ... the second train moved off ... a few minutes after the first.

The *Bolton Chronicle* (26 May 1838) waxed even more lyrical about the scenery, reporting that the Irwell flowed in 'a valley rich with the choicest beauties of rural scenery, which could only be surpassed by the Great Western Railway which runs for a considerable distance along the Valley of the Thames'.

The first train consisted solely of five first-class carriages drawn by the *Victoria*, whilst the second train consisted of one first- and four second-class carriages drawn by the *Fairfield*. The first train reached Agecroft at 11:07 a.m., Ringley at 11:16 a.m., the 'Tunnel at Clymer Clough' at 11:20 a.m., finally reaching Bolton at 11:25 a.m. Total journey time was a mere twenty-five minutes. The second-class train took thirty-eight minutes, having left Manchester 'a few minutes after eleven' and having made 'two stoppages, one of five, and the other of three minutes', making a journey time of half an hour. The reporter from the *Kendal Mercury* timed the journey of the first-class train at 26 ½ minutes precisely. One of the delays to the second-class train was 'in consequence of one of two of the axles of the carriages (which are quite new) having heated with the motion'.

First-class carriages had three six-seat compartments, and were delivered at a cost of £480 each from Melling of Manchester. Externally they were painted 'a rich lake colour', lined out in gilt with the company's arms on the door panels. The second-class carriages were rather unusual. They had a single, central door on each side and bench seats arranged along both sides and down the centre. They could accommodate thirty-two passengers and were built

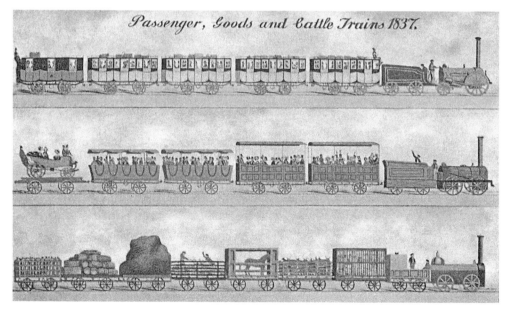

A postcard issued by the Lancashire & Yorkshire Railway in 1908 depicting travel on their system in the 1830s. (Author's Collection)

at a cost of £100 each by Mr Cooper of Bradshaw Gate, Bolton. The *Railway Times* called them a 'striking contrast to the unsightly pig-pens of the Liverpool & Manchester Railway'. Open third-class carriages were provided soon after opening in June 1838.

A 'large crowd was assembled' at Bradford Square, Bolton, to greet the first trains into the station. The return train, consisting of all ten carriages drawn by the *Victoria* departed at 12:43 p.m.:

> On reaching Farnworth, a number of proprietors got out of the carriages and walked about a mile, in order to examine the line. This caused a considerable loss of time, as did also another interruption of a similar kind at Pepper Hill, when a number got out and walked on to about Clifton Hall. These two stoppages, and a short one at Agecroft Station, occupied so much time that the train did not reach the station at Salford till ten minutes past two.

The *Kendal Mercury* added:

> The train made several stops, and the gentlemen descended from the carriages and walked for short distances along the line, inspecting the bridges, the mode of laying the rails, and other portions of the work ... The carriages stopped on their return [at] the embankment across the valley at Clifton, for the purpose of enabling the party to view, at their leisure the fine scenery on that portion of the vale of the Irwell ... The Clifton embankment commands a very favourable view of this portion of the valley.

In the evening, the directors, proprietors and guests attended a lavish dinner at Ladyman's Hotel, Bridge Street, Salford.

Rolling stock and infrastructure

The track was laid on a continuous baulk road, *à la Brunel*. Jesse Hartley had originally proposed the line be laid on a continuous bed of stone blocks, and a short portion was thus laid, but, as the *Sheffield Independent* noted in December 1837,

> An engine and carriage passed over about six miles ... the object being to try the engines and carriages over the rails, part of which are laid on *timber (Kyanized)* and part on stone. A decided preference was manifested in favour of that part laid on timber, for softness of sound and smoothness of motion, over that laid on stone, where both sound and motion were, in some degree, more rigid, but not the extent of rails laid on stone sleeps laid in the ordinary way... the rails are laid so as to maintain a uniform bearing, their whole length being a continuous bed of stone or timber, to which they are, in both instances, firmly fixed.

The rails weighed 55 lbs per yard and were laid on half baulks of timber, with cross-ties every nine feet, providing a 'very firm and substantial appearance, and the motion of the carriages ... very easy and pleasant'. The line was laid with an up and down passenger line and a third goods-only line with bi-directional working. The *Preston Chronicle* reported that the railway had some fifteen first-class carriages and twenty-two second class. They were

> Very beautiful and commodious vehicles, standing somewhat higher than those on the Liverpool and Manchester line... The second class ... are as much close carriages of the first class; the only distinction being in the absence of cushions, linings and embellishments.

The railway company also possessed six locomotives; four were 0-4-0 tender locomotives built by Edward Bury of Liverpool and named *Victoria, Fairfield, Manchester, Bolton* and two were 2-2-0 outside framed tender locomotives by Messrs. Forrester & Co. of Liverpool named *Forrester* and *Buck*. Two more 0-4-0 Bury-type locomotives were on order and 'in progress of completion' from William Fairbairn & Sons of Manchester at the time of opening. The Bury and Fairbairn locomotives were built to the same specification, with 5-foot driving wheels, 80 psi boiler, 12 x 18 inches cylinders, and weighed 10 tons 7½ cwt in working order. The two Forrester engines cost £1,050 each and had 75 psi boilers, 5-foot driving wheels, and outside cylinders measuring 11 x 18 inches. Weight in working order was 10 tons 13 cwt. Two additional locomotives – Bury 2-2-0s – were ordered in 1844 with 13 x 18 inches inside cylinders and 5-foot driving wheels. They were subsequently rebuilt as 2-2-2s.

The public opening of the railway was on Tuesday 29 May with very little ceremony. The *Blackburn Standard* reported that the first train from Manchester

> Was drawn by the *Victoria*. It started at two minutes after seven [am] with not quite a score [20] of passengers; the hour being early, and there being trains at half-past eight and

Victoria built to a standard Bury, Curtis & Kennedy design, by Fairbairn & Son for the MB&B, photographed in the 1870s. (Author's Collection)

A classic example of a Bury, Curtis & Kennedy 2-2-0, typifying Edward Bury's 'small engine' policy. (Author's Collection)

half-past nine ... The train reached Bolton about 26 minutes after seven o'clock, having performed the journey in 24 minutes ...

The first train from Bolton at seven a.m., had but few passengers. It accomplished the journey in about nineteen minutes and a half. The second train from Bolton consisted of two first-class, and three second-class carriages, all of them glass coaches, as on the Grand Junction line. It left Bolton at 28 minutes before nine o'clock with fifty-nine passengers, and reached the station, New Bailey-street, Salford, 7 minutes and a half before nine o'clock.

Sadly, the opening week was marred by a fatal accident the day before the opening. It was, opined the local press, the result of 'indiscrete and careless conduct on the part of the deceased':

It seems that a train had brought up a number of persons from Manchester, and amongst them some joiners who had been working on the line. When near Bolton, the engine was stopped for some purpose; and during the stoppage the deceased and some of his shop-mates commenced bustling and jostling each other in fun. This play ended in the deceased being precipitated off the lorry on which they were frolicking. He fell on the road and was so severely injured that he died almost immediately.

Terminal Stations

The station at New Bailey Street, Salford – now part of Salford Central – was

A neat building, conveniently situated in a great public thoroughfare. Ascending by a wide staircase (after providing himself with his ticket), the passenger will find himself

A late Victorian print of Salford Central Station, or as it was originally known, New Bailey Street. Opened by the MB&B in 1838. (Author's Collection)

considerably elevated above the streets on either side, the railway being raised on massive arches, which are about to be converted into spacious warehouses for the reception of chiefly cotton goods ... and doubtless amongst other praiseworthy orders and regulations, he will not fail to remark on the extreme civility of the company's servants.

The railway ran on a massive, thirty-eight-arch brick viaduct some 444 yards long, 'between warehouses and walls, and the usual thronging of bricks and mortar'. Wishaw noted that the main building was 78 feet long and 30 feet wide and presented 'a neat elevation'.

From the passage in front of the booking office a flight of stairs leads up to the arrival and departure platforms. The egress for arrival passengers is by distinct staircases, which lead out into the street under the end arches of the viaduct. The platforms are arranged on either side of the railway, and are continued at the end next the offices. There are altogether five lines of way at this station; the whole, except for the front office, being raised on a viaduct.

Trains from the MB&B were able to work into Victoria from July 1843 with the opening of the 728-foot-long, 27-foot-wide iron colonnade, designed by Hawkshaw, to link to the L&M extension to Victoria Station. It was supported on one side by the station viaduct, and on the other by iron columns along the centre of Upper Booth Street. It was built at a cost of £10,500. New Bailey Street became a through station in 1863 following the construction

The same view over a century later; the elegant cast iron parapets were much criticised when new. (Author)

Main entrance to Salford Central in 2016: note the unusual Egyptian-style cast-iron columns. (Author)

Above: An early colour postcard by the Lancashire & Yorkshire Railway depicting Trinity Street Station *c*. 1900. (Author's Collection)

Left: All that remains of the L&Y station today is the impressive clock tower. (Author)

of an iron viaduct running parallel on the north side of the LNWR line, with iron bridges across the Irwell and Great Ducie Street. This viaduct was constructed at a cost of £203,370.

The station at Bolton was squeezed between Trinity Street (north), Manchester Street (east) and Bridgeman Street (south). It was bounded on the west by Trinity Church. The station layout had five tracks, each ending in a turntable, and there was a single, canopied island platform 11 feet wide. Engine sheds were built at Salford and Bolton (location unknown).

Wishaw continues:

> At the Bolton terminus the office are likewise placed across the end of the railway, but are nearly on the level of the rails; and the approach from the street to the booking-office is be a descending flight of steps ... three of the lines are covered by a queen-post wooden roof, supported on iron columns; this roof projects over one of the passenger platforms; and on the other side of the double main way, the platform ... is enclosed behind with a brick wall; and the whole is covered with a sloping roof, the front of which is supported on iron columns. The goods-depot, on rather a large scale, is contiguous to this station.

It became a through-station in 1848 when the Bolton & Preston Railway was opened; the Blackburn, Darwen & Bolton opened in the same year, having to tunnel under the street. Bolton station was enlarged in 1871 by extending the platforms to the north, around the curves to Preston to the north-west and Blackburn to the north-east. In 1877 Bridgeman Street bridge was closed and demolished, opening up the southern approach to the station; Trinity Street and Orland Street bridges were widened at the same time to compensate for the loss of the Bridgeman Street bridge. A triangular junction – 'Johnson Street Fork' – was

Interior of Trinity Street in steam days. (Author's Collection)

A much-reduced Trinity Street in 2016. (Author)

opened in 1888 allowing trains from Preston to run through to Blackburn and vice versa. Finally, in 1904, the station was completely rebuilt, with two island platforms running north to south from Trinity to Orlando Street. The 1904 buildings were demolished in the 1980s and Bolton Station underwent considerable modernisation from 2005 to 2006, and a new 'Bolton Transport Interchange' was opened in 2010.

Operations

From 1838 to 1846 the MB&B drove on the right, which naturally caused considerable apprehension amongst the first passengers; one of whom

> Put his head out of the window and called loudly to the Guard, asking him if the train was not on the wrong line. He was speedily assured that all was right, and that there was no fear of a collision ... the "rule of the road" on this railway one is the *pedestrian* rather than the *carriage* rule. The trains take their right side rail; those going from Manchester going on the east and those from Bolton on the west side of the line. This is contrary to the custom and on the Liverpool & Manchester and Grand Junction, London & Birmingham, and other lines ...
>
> (*Manchester Courier* 2 June 1838)

The first timetable of May 1838 indicates that trains left from either terminal of the line at the same times, clearly catering for the business commuter, with trains departing at: 7:00 a.m.; 8:30 a.m.; 9:30 a.m.; 12 noon; 3:00 p.m.; 5:00 p.m.; and 7:00 p.m. By October, the *Bolton Chronicle* stated that the MB&B was 'doing an immense business in Passengers'. In order to capitalise on this 'immense business', enterprising hoteliers – as in Manchester – began to direct their advertising to passengers:

Lever's Arms Hotel.
Nelson Square, Bolton.
M. Mascall
Grateful for the practical support he has received since he entered upon the above Premises, begs to inform his friends and the Public, that the LEVER'S ARMS is the nearest HOTEL to the STATION of the MANCHESTER, BOLTON, & BURY RAILWAY, being only two minutes walk from it.
NB Excellent Stabling, Good Beds, Choice Wines.

The proprietor of the Bolton's leading hotel, The Commercial – which also boasted its own Assembly Rooms – similarly advertised towards railway passengers, having 'excellent beds ... wine of a superior quality, excellent stabling and Coach House' and 'situated in a direct line from the Railway Station, and is placed in the most central part of town'.

The train times were revised within a week of opening, on Monday 11 June 1838, providing ten trains in each direction daily and two each way on Sundays:

First Train, Seven A.M. – stopping at
Pendleton Bridge,
Dixon Fold Bridge   } Stations
Seddon's Fold Bridge, Kearsley

Second Train, Eight A.M. *not* stopping on the road
Third Train, Nine A.M. stopping at the stations
Fourth Train, Ten A.M. *not* stopping on the road
Fifth Train, Twelve Noon, stopping at the stations
Sixth Train, Half-past Two P.M., *not* stopping on the road
Seventh Train, Four P.M. stopping at the stations
Eighth Train, Five P.M. *not* stopping at the stations
Ninth Train, Six PM, stopping at the stations
Tenth Train, Seven PM, *not* stopping on the road

On Sundays, Manchester to Bolton
First Train, Eight A.M. stopping at the stations
Second Train, Six P.M. stopping at the stations

From Bolton to Manchester
First Train, Nine A.M. stopping at the stations
Second Train, Seven P.M. stopping at the stations.

Unlike on other lines, trains were run mixed, with a first-class fare costing 2s 6d, second class 2s and 'open carriages' 1s 6d. Children under seven years of age travelled half-price. A revised timetable was issued in June 1839 in the light of the first twelve months of operation: ten trains a day, but with the train at 11 am rather than 12 noon, 1.30 pm rather than 2.0 pm and 4.0 pm rather than 3.0 pm, still clearly catering for commuters travelling on business. A twelve-train service was introduced from 21 August 1840 'to meet Trains to and from Stockport'. From the same date, the cost of the 'open cars' was reduced to 1s, attached to two trains during the day with a special worker's train in the evening:

	Fares		
	Covered Cars		Open Cars
	First Class	Second	
7 o'clock, Morning, not stopping	2s 6d	1s 6d	-
8 o'clock, Morning, stopping at the stations	2s 6d	1s 6d	1s
9 o'clock, Morning, not stopping	2s 6d	1s 6d	-
10 o'clock, Morning, stopping at the stations	2s 6d	1s 6d	-
11 o'clock, Morning, not stopping	2s 6d	1s 6d	-
12 o'clock, Afternoon, stopping at the stations	2s 6d	1s 6d	1s
2 o'clock. Afternoon, stopping at the stations	2s 6d	1s 6d	-
4 o'clock, Afternoon, not stopping	2s 6d	1s 6d	-
5 o'clock, Afternoon, stopping at the stations	2s 6d	1s 6d	-
6 o'clock, Afternoon, not stopping	2s 6d	1s 6d	-
7 o'clock, Afternoon, stopping at the stations	2d 6d	1s 6d	-
7 ¾ o'clock, Afternoon, stopping at the stations	-	-	1s

A colour Lancashire & Yorkshire Railway postcard of Farnworth, c. 1910. (Author's Collection)

Farnworth Station in 2016, following the remodelling of the route for the proposed electrification of the Salford – Preston route. (Author)

Moses Gate, *c.* 1910, in an early colour postcard issued by the Lancashire & Yorkshire Railway. (Author's Collection)

Moses Gate over a century later. (Author)

Special trains were also provided during the 'Manchester Races Week' at Kersal Moor, from 1838. By 1845 they ran from Bolton to Agecroft Bridge Station hourly, from 10:30 a.m. until 2:30 p.m. and 'commencing again so soon as the Races are over'. Fares 'Open Boxes 1s, Closed Carriages 1s 6d.' Stations at Farnworth – known as Tunnel station – and Moses Gate were opened by 1843; Tunnel station became 'Halshaw Moor' in 1845, subsequently 'Farnworth and Halshaw Moor.'

Accidents and Felonies

A year after the opening of the line, there was a fatal accident when the *Woolton* 'a new Engine ... by Mr William Fairbairn' over-turned in the Farnworth tunnel, killing her crew. The 'usual nine o'clock morning train from Bolton ... and consisted ... of two second-class carriages, two first-class carriages and a goods waggon' carrying about twenty-eight passengers. 'About three hundred yards' on the 'Bolton side of the tunnel' the guard heard

A grinding noise for which he could not account, and he examined, as well as he was able, during the running of the train, but was unable to perceive anything wrong about the wheels or axles of the carriages. He next perceived the speed of the train was slackened; and on upon re-ascending to his seat ... he perceived the engine turned upside down, and immediately afterwards, the concussion from the carriage on which he was sat, he was hurled from his seat, and fell upon the engine ... the passengers were safe, though of course much frightened and shaken, some of them also having received contusions from the shock.

(Leeds Times 15 June 1839).

The guard then made his way toward the engine and could find neither the engineman (Richard Purdie) nor fireman (David Cavanagh). A search was then made inside the tunnel and

The engineer was found on the spot where he had been thrown when the engine overturned, at a distance of about fifteen yards from it, his thigh having been broken in the fall. He was taken up in great agony, and nearly insensible, and was promptly removed to Bolton, to his lodgings ... under the care of Mr Hampson, surgeon, who set the fractured limb ... At first the poor fireman Cavanagh could not be found; but at length the tender, which had been overturned, was raised, and his body was found lying across the rails, life being quite extinct ... the body was conveyed to the St John's Tavern, Halshaw Moor.

The accident appears to have been caused by either damaged 'shunt or switch, a few yards from the entrance of the tunnel, on the Bolton side, which was placed there temporarily, for the convenience of moving rubbish'. The switch had been out of use for 'three weeks' and the 'tongue ... was locked in such a position as to render it impossible that it could move, or that the wheels of the carriages ... could come nearer than three

Clifton Junction around 1900; the line to Bury closed in 1966. (Author's Collection)

Clifton Junction station in 2016: Clifton is one of the least used stations in Britain. In 2014 to 2015 it saw only 152 passengers – it's easy to see why. (Author)

inches'. After the accident, the 'tongue ... was found lying loose' and 'lying in a sloping direction across the outer rail, the bolt which passed through the tongue near its centre, having been broken'. The *Manchester Guardian* suggested that the breaking of this bolt may have been malicious given 'the breaking of this bolt ... could not have been effected but by the application of considerable force'. John Betley, a weaver, was killed at Stoneclough station by falling onto the line from the footpath which ran alongside on 12 January 1842; 'in endeavouring to get out the way of the train ... was knocked down, the wheels passing over both his legs'. James Cooke, a passenger guard, was killed at Kearsley Bridge on 26 July 1844:

> For some cause or another, he put his head out the right hand side of the carriage; the passengers supposed that he was looking to see whether the brake operated; but, unfortunately, the train at that moment passed under the bridge by which the Kearsley and Ringley road is carried over the line; this bridge is supported on wooden piers; and the head of the deceased came violently into contact with one of these piers. The concussion was such as to immediately deprive him of life.
>
> (*Manchester Courier* 27 July 1844)

John Ryder, one of the firemen, was killed in a collision between two trains on the curve between Dixon Green and Stoneclough station on 5 July 1845:

In consequence in repairs of the rails on the west side from this town [Bolton], both engines had to run on one line of rail. Both of the engine-tenders were ... aware ... and particular instructions were given to the engineers for their guidance; they believed that they would be able to meet at such a point as one would go on the opposite line whilst the other passed ... where the accident occurred there is a severe curve, so that neither of the drivers were able to see the other's approach at any great distance...

(*Bolton Chronicle* 12 July 1845)

William Williams, who was taking a locomotive light engine from Manchester to Bolton, however, despite receiving instructions from the Station Master in Manchester that he 'had to go on the left hand line (the one under repair) to the Kearsley "shunt" and remain there' until the train from Bolton had passed, 'very foolishly disobeyed his instructions' and collided head-on with the Bolton train. The driver of the Bolton train, James Tonge, whose colleague Ryder was, noted:

In some way or another ... [John Ryder] had got between the two lines and was lying there quite dead ... When the engines came into contact, that which met us was driven some little distance and then both came to a stand. The engine and tender were much broken by the shock, and the water tank of the latter flew over my head after I had jumped off ... William Williams was the driver of the engine ... and Joseph Allen was the fireman and both jumped off, and Williams received severe injuries ...

Joseph Allen, the other fireman, believed that the accident had occurred due to the watchman, Frederick Bloomfield, at 'Kearsley shunt' telling him that 'Tonge ... would either stay at Bolton or be on a good look-out in the keeping out of the way' and it was safe for Williams to proceed. Bloomfield, however, denied this, stating that he did not know where Tonge and his train were. A jury finally recorded 'accidental death'.

Samuel Heywood, a thirty-six-year-old clerk at New Bailey Street station was charged and transported for ten years after admitting to embezzling £50 in the new year of 1842. Heywood had been in debt to the tune of £1,200 and had attempted to flee to America, having left a letter to his wife admitting his guilt. He was arrested on a ship bound for Philadelphia from Liverpool, a week later.

The Battle of Clifton Junction

The MB&B became part of the Lancashire & Yorkshire system in 1847 and relationships with the neighbouring East Lancashire Railway, which had running rights on the MB&B from New Bailey Street to Clifton Junction, became increasingly strained. The L&Y charged tolls for every passenger and ton of freight which passed over its own metals, and for several years this worked easily enough. The problems started, however, when the ELR began to run express trains from New Bailey Street which did not stop at Clifton Junction (where the L&Y official were able to check ELR tickets and freight dockets). The L&Y demanded that ELR trains had to stop at Clifton so tickets could be checked; the ELR in reply refused. Thus, on 12 March 1849, when the first ELR express from Manchester arrived at Clifton Junction at 10:30 a.m., the driver was forced to stop as his way had been blocked by heavy baulks of timber placed across the line by L&Y platelayers. L&Y staff then demanded a full ticket inspection but the ELR guard refused, as, according to his own regulations, tickets had been collected at Radcliffe. Sensing trouble he alerted the police and large detachments arrived from Bury and Pendleton.

The L&Y then brought up an empty passenger train with the intention of taking on the ELR passengers; ELR men removed the baulks of timber, and then moved up their train so that the two were touching buffers. A 'Push of war' ensued; each engine driver trying to force the other to retire. Neither made any progress, but the ELR retaliated by bringing up a goods train loaded with stone. By midday, no fewer than eight rival trains were blocking the junction, and the presence of the police did little to reduce tensions. Henry Blackmore, the L&Y Passenger Superintendent, defused the situation – perhaps sensing events had gone on for long enough – and ordered the L&Y to back down and let the ELR train proceed. As a result the ELR proposed its own line to Manchester via Whitefield and Cheetham Hill, which caused the L&Y to capitulate at this threat to loss of traffic, and the line between Manchester and Clifton Junction, was to be jointly vested in the two companies as the Clifton & Manchester Railway.

CHAPTER 3

The Manchester & Leeds Railway (1840)

The first proposal for a trans-Pennine railway linking Manchester with Leeds came in 1825. As with many other railway schemes of this period it was born out of dissatisfaction with the various canal companies and as a means of challenging their monopoly on bulk, long-distance transport. Sadly, due to the financial situation of 1825–1826 (severe depression), the scheme never materialised, but the idea of crossing the Pennines by rail was sown and the second scheme was drafted in 1830; a public meeting being held in Manchester less than a month after the opening of the Liverpool & Manchester. The 'Manchester & Leeds Railway Company' was formally organised with a share capital of £800,000 in £100 shares. George Stephenson and George Walker were appointed as engineers. Walker proposed forming an end-on junction with the L&M

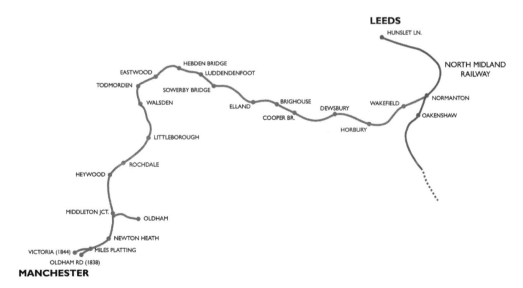

Map of the Manchester & Leeds Railway, and its connection to Leeds via the North Midland. (Andy Mason)

at Liverpool Road and carrying his line through Manchester to Ashton-under-Lyne, Mossley, Uppermill, passing along Broadhead Dale, tunnelling into the Dean Head Valley and then to Brighouse, connecting with the proposed Bradford & Leeds Railway. Stephenson, however, proposed a far more circuitous route via the Calder Valley, which was longer but easier and cheaper to construct. The Bill was introduced to Parliament on 28 February 1831. It received its second reading in March but it was held up by opposition from the Rochdale Canal Company, and any further progress was stopped by the dissolution of Parliament in April. The Bill was re-introduced in June 1831 and considered by committee over the summer but was thrown out.

The businessmen of Leeds and Manchester, however, were not so easily deterred. A third scheme was promoted in 1835. At a meeting in Manchester on 21 October 1835, the company was reconstituted with capital fixed at £800,000; in the following year George Stephenson was appointed engineer. Thomas Longridge Gooch was appointed as his assistant. Stephenson still envisaged a route through the Calder Valley with two tunnels, the longest being the 1,705-yard-long Summit Tunnel near Littleborough. Beyond Sowerby Bridge the line would descend toward Wakefield and join the projected North Midland Railway at Normanton. The Bill was introduced in February 1836 and faced fierce opposition from the canal companies and landed gentry. Henry Clarkson, one of Stephenson's assistants who surveyed and staked out the line through Wakefield, recalled in his memoirs how he was chased off land by dogs and threatened with arrest by disgruntled land-owners.

The first public meeting of the Company was held in the Town Hall, King Street, Manchester in January 1836, chaired by the Borough reeve and attended by

The Cathedral-like Todmorden Unitarian Church, paid for by John Fielden in 1865 at a cost of £353,000 (over £3 million in today's prices). (Author)

Mark Philips MP (a prominent and extremely wealthy Unitarian mill-owner), various members of the Potter family, Robert Garnett (a wealthy Unitarian Manchester merchant), and J. P. Westhead (MP for Knaresborough and future Chairman of the M&B). The first general meeting was held in September of the same year: James Wood was appointed Chairman, and J. D. Barry, secretary. Amongst the committee were Thomas Potter, John Fielden (MP for Oldham), James Fielden, and Henry Tootal (a prominent corn merchant of Wakefield). The Fieldens were wealthy Unitarian mill owners in Todmorden; John Fielden was instrumental in the passing of the Factory Act (1847), which restricted working hours for women and young people in the mills to ten hours.

The proposed capital of the new company was £1,300,000 and a finance committee was appointed to raise this amount. The proposed expense of construction was estimated to be £948,482, and receipts were predicted at £115,256 for passenger traffic and £113,707 for freight per annum. Freight was envisaged as being cotton and linens from Manchester travelling east to Leeds and then onwards – via the Leeds & Selby Railway – to the Humber and then Hull. Woollens and coal travelling west to Manchester and thence Liverpool and finally corn from the West Riding – centred on Wakefield, where an impressive Corn Exchange was finished in 1837 – going in either direction. Wakefield was also the scene of fierce disputes between the Aire & Calder Navigation Company and also between the townsmen and the railway company over the construction of the eleven-arch Calder Valley Viaduct through that town. Whilst the M&L was still going through Parliament, wealthy corn merchants and wool-staplers of Wakefield, Leeds, and Pontefract – chaired by Lord Hawke of Womersley Hall – established the Manchester, Leeds & Goole Railway to extend the Manchester & Leeds and North Midland via Pontefract and Snaith, to Goole. The new line would shave 25 miles off the journey to the Humber. This would later re-emerge as the Wakefield, Pontefract & Goole Railway, opened in 1848.

The proprietors received Royal Assent on 4 July 1836. The Act authorised a joint stock capital of £1.3 million and an additional £433,000 could be raised by loans. There was an additional proviso that if the North Midland Railway had not been completed in time for the M&L to join it at Normanton, then the M&L was authorised to construct its own line from Normanton to Leeds. Work started on the line in August 1837, from Manchester to Littleborough. Daniel Gooch, the brother of Thomas Longridge Gooch, was appointed as his assistant responsible for the Rochdale section and Barnard Dickinson was appointed assistant engineer responsible for the Summit Tunnel in January 1838.

A Board of Directors was elected from shareholders and, to 'secure a broad representation of interest local to the line' of the twenty-nine, ten were to be residents of Manchester, eight residents of Leeds, four of Liverpool, three of Halifax, two of Bradford and one of Todmorden. The chairman was Henry Houldsworth Esq. of Manchester. He was a wealthy Unitarian cotton spinner; his son, Sir William Henry Houldsworth, would continue the family business and build what was then the largest cotton spinning mill in the world at Reddish, near Stockport, in 1865. He would, however, turn his back and repudiate his father's theology and Liberal politics, becoming a 'High Churchman' and Tory. Houldsworth and Fielden both sat on the railway's Management Sub-Committee. Captain John Milligen Laws RN, of Ardwick House, Manchester, was appointed general manager. Laws, the nephew of Sir Robert Sannard, Surveyor to the Navy, had had a distinguished career during the Napoleonic Wars and later commanded the fifty-two-gun HMS *Southampton*. As a qualified civil engineer, this placed him in good stead for supervising the building of the line.

Another naval officer, Commander – later Admiral – Cheesman Henry Binstead, was appointed as 'traffic and passenger superintendent' in 1842. Binstead had previously served as 'Agent for Transports Afloat' (1828–34), coordinating the troop ships that carried British soldiers and materiel around the globe, giving him good experience of managing traffic patterns. He had temporary command of HMS *Spitfire* (1841), a wooden paddle gunboat. Binstead would be employed Lancashire & Yorkshire Railway until 1871. He was a Director of the Wakefield, Pontefract & Goole Railway and major shareholder of the L&Y. He died in 1876, aged 79.

The *Leeds Mercury* declared the M&L to be

> One of the great and important lines of railway communication ... radiating from this great metropolis of manufacturers, perhaps one of the most valuable and important will be that which connects the capital of cotton with the capital of woollen manufacture ... the line will form one grand connecting link in the great chain of railway communication which is rapidly bringing Manchester into closer communication – we might say almost contact – with hitherto distant places. Not only does it connect the eastern and western shores of our Island ... but it forms a junction with the great eastern line of railway [i.e. the Great Northern] from London northward to Scotland...

The two major engineering feats were the Summit Tunnel at Littleborough and the embankment spanning the Irk Valley near Middleton. Stone viaducts were built at Todmordern of nine arches (seven of 60-ft and two of 30-ft span and 54 feet 6 inches high); Charlestown (three arches); Elland; Horbury and Wakefield (sixteen arches). Contracts were advertised throughout 1837 and 1838. Compensation to land owners totalled £146,448 but the Company only paid out £44,628.

Nowt So Queer As Folk

There was considerable opposition to the railway, not only from the canal interests, but from land owners and even towns which were reluctant to have a railway pass through them.

Despite being shareholders and directors of the Company, the Fieldens of Todmorden were eager to extract the maximum amount of compensation from the loss of their land to the railway. The Fieldens – Joshua, John, James and Thomas – were hugely influential Unitarian mill-owners and parliamentarians. They built the magnificent Unitarian Church in Todmorden in 1865 and also the Town Hall. For a strip of land 300 yards long and 50 feet wide, the Fieldens claimed compensation totalling £1,819 13s 10d. According to the *Manchester Courier*, the court proceedings took two days:

> The jury, after nearly and hour's consultation, gave their verdict ... land and buildings and timber, £1,191 10s 6d; severance, including £55 mill damages, £215.

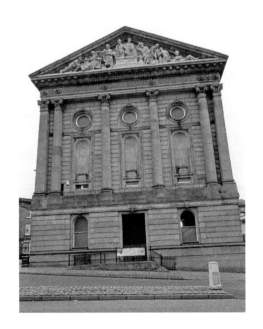

Another legacy of the Fieldens: Todmorden Town Hall completed in 1875 and given to the town. (Author)

At nearby Sowerby Bridge, Samuel Turner claimed £1,500 from the company in compensation for 'a valuable stone quarry'; the Company offered £500 – the value of the land. Again the dispute went to court and the jury decided that the company should only pay Turner £475, and that Turner also had to pay the costs.

No doubt goaded by the Calder & Hebble Navitagion Co., and a local but inert aristocracy – who were implacably opposed to the M&L – the townsfolk of Wakefield attempted to prevent the passage of the railway close to the town. In May 1838 there were disputes over land in Thornes (just south of the town) and Kirkthorpe (to the east). Again, the matter went to court, but in this instance the jury found in favour of the Company, much to the fury of the local press. But worse was to come; the M&L Act gave it the right to construct a viaduct and station at or near Kirkgate, which was to be crossed by a bridge. An injunction was placed on the railway company, however, over the claim that the company was in breach of its own Act because the bridge crossing Kirkgate had two of its piers occupying part of the highway, reducing its width from 34 feet to 30. Matters became so heated that some of the infuriated townsfolk expected the Company to demolish the viaduct. The matter was the subject of expensive litigation for over two years, eventually reaching the Court of Chancery, in London, in 1840.

Part of the viaduct collapsed early in November 1839 killing James Williams, one of the workers. Henry Clarkson, the surveyor of the M&L from Todmorden to Leeds recalled:

On the 8th November 1838, I was walking to Wakefield from Sandal with my Clerk, William Paley, and had almost reached the recently formed viaduct across the Ings Road, at the moment that a heavy train of loaded wagons, drawn by horses, was passing over it. Just before we reached it, I saw the sides of the arch suddenly give way; the centre rise up, and then fall in a confused mass ... The man in charge of the wagons and the horses was killed and the Inspector of the works had a very narrow escape, being only saved by my shouting loudly to him ...

Wakefield Kirkgate, originally built by the Great Northern and Lancashire & Yorkshire as a joint station in 1854 (replacing an earlier structure of 1840), after its multi-million-pound facelift. (Paul Dawson)

Undaunted by this tragedy or the legal case, the Company pushed on with rebuilding the viaduct; much to the disgust of the Tory, Anglican *Wakefield Journal*:

> Workmen are completing the viaduct over Kirkgate ... we *presume* that some arrangement has been entered into between the contending parties ... We have understood that the case was not to have been settled ...

The station at Wakefield was built at Kirkgate on a plot formerly occupied by strawberry fields and Aspdin's cement works. The original timber structure was replaced by the L&Y and the Great Northern in 1854 with a magnificent stone station. In 2013–15, after many years of neglect, Wakefield Kirkgate was restored at a cost of £4 million to breathe new life into the building which, since the 1970s – despite being the larger of Wakefield's two stations – was unmanned, unsafe, and virtually derelict.

There was further trouble crossing the River Calder at Broad Reach, to the north-east of Wakefield. The Company announced in January 1839 that it was to divert the route of the river 'near to Kirkthorpe, in the parishes of Warmfield and Wakefield'. The Company had initially planned to cross the Calder by three bridges but, to reduce the cost of building the line, a single three-arch skew bridge and embankment was created, which required the re-routing of the Calder. Several wealthy Wakefield landowners blocked this move, claiming that the plans of this work had not been submitted to the Navigation Company for perusal and had a stop placed on the work. The local press announced 'Stoppage of work at Wakefield' until the matter could be resolved; the Railway Company eventually paying some £12,352 to the canal interests to enable the diversion of the Calder at Broad Reach. The new 'cut' for the Calder was in fact beneficial to the canal companies, as it shortened and straightened the Calder. However, as it happened, it was ultimately of little benefit as the Aire & Calder Navigation opened its own cut between Broad Reach Stanley Ferry, effectively bypassing the cut dug by the railway. Furthermore, the local newspapers were far from impressed at the arrival of the railway navvies:

> There are at present in Wakefield and the Neighbourhood, a great number of "navigators", of whom no favourable opinion is entertained.
>
> (*Leeds Mercury* 12 January 1839)

These various land disputes severely impeded the progress of the line; a situation made worse through various labour disputes.

Summit Tunnel

The Summit Tunnel at Littleborough was the major engineering feat of the M&L. The work commenced on the tunnel in January 1838 with the digging of a series of ten shafts along the centre line of the tunnel; the first bricks were laid in No. 10 Shaft on 17 August 1838 by the Chairman, James Woods, and it was completed by 8 November. Some twenty huts were built by the Company for the Navvies; by 1841 there were seventy-five 'for the dwellings

Summit Tunnel, once the longest in Britain, is still as dark and forbidding as when it was opened in 1841. (Author)

for the work people'. Given that several hundreds of men were employed, these huts can only have been for the foremen, overlookers, and other important employees. Many more of the workers 'built for themselves about 100 huts on the Summit, above the tunnel'.

There was constant feuding between the English and Irish Navvies – often leading to pitched battles on the moors and even in the streets of towns. The *Halifax Guardian* reported in August 1839:

> On Monday last, the peaceful town of Hebden Bridge ... was thrown into the greatest state of Alarm by a number of the excavators from the works of Messr. Moss and Taylor, running through the town in the wildest confusion, pursued by about double their number of railwaymen, armed with pick-shafts, picks, shovels, &c., hallooing and shouting "down with 'em,", "down with 'em." These latter were English, who had united to drive all the Irish from the Line; they then drove them completely out of the town ... vowing and swearing death to any Irishman they should find. Having, as they thought, completely ousted the Irish, the conquerors then returned in a body to return to the line to stop the whole of the men remaining at work; in order, as they said, to go with them to the adjoining contracts throughout Calderdale, and drive every Irishman off the works.

Mr Moss (of Moss and Taylor) called for the magistrates, the police, and a troop of Dragoons from Todmorden who, 'drawn up in front of the works with drawn swords', suitably cowed the malcontents, who returned to work. In September 1839 the 'determined' Constable Daniel Mackintyre was sent to Todmorden to arrest one 'Donnelly, a workman on the Manchester & Leeds Railway' for 'neglect of family'. Upon arresting Donnelly, he broke free and 'took refuge behind the gang, most of whom lifted up their spades and picks and threatened to murder the constable', whereupon Mackintyre

> Drew a brace of pistols, and advancing towards his prisoner, said he would shoot the first man who offered to resist him: the overlooker then interfered and persuaded the men to let Donnelly be taken, and he was secured and brought before the Magistrates at Rochdale.
> (*Leeds Times* 28 September 1839)

The troubles continued into the following year: in March 1840 the *Manchester Guardian* reported that sixteen workmen had been charged with intimidating their fellows to throw them off the works. These workmen 'seriously annoyed 32 labourers who had lately arrived from North Shields and who were engaged for six months at 5s per day'. The 'Old Hands' gathered and attempted to intimidate the Tynesiders from turning up to work, even offering 35s if they stayed away. John Stephenson, the Contractor, had the men brought before the Rochdale Magistrates and six of the sixteen 'conspirators' were sentenced to three months' hard labour. In 1840 there was a 'turn out' amongst the bricklayers, and Gooch introduced a bonus scheme to encourage the workmen and speed up the rate of progress.

With all the labour disputes, work on the tunnel was not progressing as rapidly as the Directors wanted:

> The tunnel at the summit ... it not being proceeded with as rapidly as the contractors ought ... some changes must be immediately made as regards to the number of men

The impressive iron viaduct over the canal at Gawksholme. (Author)

Rail meets road and river at Littleborough. (Author)

employed, and the general management of the work. If a sufficient number of men be employed, there can be no difficulty in completing the tunnel in the year 1840.

(The Railway Times 30 March 1839).

The last brick of the tunnel lining was laid on 9 December 1840 and it was inspected by Gooch, who was confident the line would be open throughout on 21 December. But, there was a final eleventh-hour obstacle; press reports began circulating that part of the tunnel had collapsed, the *Manchester Guardian* noting that 'Some excitement was caused upon the Manchester Exchange', based upon what appeared to be exaggerated rumours of the collapse. It noted:

> We find, however, upon inquiry ... though there has been a partial failure of a portion of the tunnel [some reports stated as much as 500 yards had collapsed], it is by no means of so serious a character as was first represented ... We believe it is the opinion of the engineer that the defective portion of the arch will have to be removed, which will probably occupy four or five weeks.

(Manchester Guardian 19 December 1840)

What had happened was that soft ground at the bottom of the tunnel had shifted, causing one of the inverts, which supported the vaulting of the tunnel, to subside. Stephenson and Gooch reported to the Directors that work would be promptly put in hand, and in total some 120 yards of the damaged invert were repaired and strengthened. A new date for the public opening was announced: 1 March 1841.

Summit Tunnel was the scene of a dreadful accident in spring 1846. A heavy goods train, drawn by the *Cleckheaton*, was heading from Manchester to Leeds, entering the tunnel at 11:45 a.m., but 'upon arriving near the centre of the summit' found that due to greasy rails

Todmorden Viaduct as depicted by A. F. Tait in 1845. (Author's Collection)

The same view 170 years later. (Author)

> He could make very little progress ... Fearing lest the twelve o'clock passenger train should arrive whilst he was in the tunnel, and a collision ensue, [the engineman] sent back the Guard (a man of the name of James Morgan) with a red signal and torches to stop the approaching train; in going back, Morgan did not obey his instructions, but got upon the wrong line. The *up mail train* was passing through the tunnel nearly at the same time, and struck Morgan, leaving him a corpse on the spot. Consequently there was no red signal to be seen; and a few minutes after the passenger train from Manchester came up and ran at speed into the luggage train, throwing the engine and one wagon off the line, but inflicting no injury whatever on the passengers.
>
> (*Leeds Intelligencer* 14 March 1846)

Luckily, Captain Binstead, the superintendent, had been at Littleborough, and 'lost little time in procuring torches and proceeding with every platelayer' into the tunnel to the aid of the wrecked trains, whilst placing red signals on the up and down lines 'to prevent any engine from coming into the tunnel, until a safe arrangement could be adopted'. The tunnel was cleared by 7 p.m. During the subsequent inquest, Binstead was praised for his quick thinking; a deodand of one shilling was placed upon the *Cleckheaton* and a verdict of accidental death was recorded for Morgan.

Manchester Oldham Road

Manchester's third railway station – now demolished – was on Oldham Road, on the outskirts of the city. Work commenced on the contract in summer 1837. A fifty-eight-arch brick viaduct approached the elevated station, 730 yards long. The station and viaduct was

Manchester Oldham Road, built by the Manchester & Leeds Railway in 1838, *c.* 1900. (National Railway Museum/Science & Society Picture Library)

across land owned by the Earl of Derby and the Earl of Ducie; the latter was already laying out his land in building plots and was eager to improve the poor road communications in that part of the town. Derby left his agents in charge of land negotiations and they were 'able to bring railway companies to advantageous terms'. There were, however, difficulties with the nearby Roman Catholic School in Oldham Road. The Company required 267 yards of land owned by the school, and offered them £111 for the value of the land, but nothing in compensation. This high-handed approach backfired with the Railway eventually having to pay nearly £500 to the school.

Due to the steep incline of the viaduct into Manchester, locomotives were detached at Miles Platting and trains worked down to the station by gravity and hauled back up using a stationary winding engine. The *Rules and Regulations* for the Manchester & Leeds stated that no engine was to pass onto the head of the incline plane into Manchester and Enginemen were to be constantly alert for the signal lamps at that point. The new station was described by Francis Wishaw:

There are several lines of way at this station, which is entirely elevated on arches. The passenger-shed is covered with a wooden roof in two spans. The booking-office is on the ground floor; and the passenger platform is approached by a flight of forty-five steps, each of 7 ½ inches rise. The whole length of the station is 176 yards and the width 80 yards.

The locomotive engine-house, which is removed to a little distance of the station, is of polygonal form, according to Mr Stephenson's usual plan.

The engine shed at Oldham Road was built in a triangle of land between the mainline to Oldham Road and the later Hunt's Bank extension. It was a roundhouse with a turntable supplied by Messrs. Bowden & Edwards.

The arches under the viaduct carrying the station and approach lines were used to store goods and merchandise at a low level, but given the 'immense quantities of goods' received and despatched from Oldham Road, this presented another set of problems. *The Railway Times* reported in April 1841 that a steam powered wagon lift, designed by Stephenson himself, had been installed to ease transhipment from high to low level:

> The Directors have spared no expense ... A steam engine has been erected ... but instead of raising each single bale or cask [as done with the hand cranes], a waggon is loaded beneath with its full complement of goods, back-sheeted, &c., ready to start for its destination.

In the same month a young apprentice caused an accident when he climbed onboard an unattended locomotive – strictly contrary to regulation – that had arrived from Leeds with a luggage train. Not only had the engineman contravened regulation by leaving the

Remains of the massive viaduct leading toward Oldham Road. (Author)

locomotive unattended, he had also left it in gear, and with the brakes off. *The Railway Times* (24 April 1841) describes what happened next:

> Probably not understanding the engine, the boy set it in motion, and it darted forward, broke through the wall of the shed, and fell a height of about 20 feet into the field below … It lay there until about six o'clock the next morning when it was got out, and it appeared that the damage done … was very trifling.

Luckily, the apprentice had 'got off the engine' and escaped with no harm, but 'has not been seen since'.

Given its out-of-the-way location, the fate of Oldham Road was sealed in 1839, less than a year after opening, when the M&L obtained an Act to extend its line through to Hunt's Bank, to build a more central station and, it was hoped, to join up with the L&M to provide through-running from Liverpool to Leeds and thence the Humber at Selby – the issue of different gauges notwithstanding. The L&M was laid at a gauge of 4 feet 8 ½ inches whilst the M&L was 4 feet 9 inches. Oldham Road closed to passengers in 1844 and became a goods station. It was finally closed and demolished in 1968. Most of the site is now a Royal Mail sorting office and an Oriental cash and carry supermarket.

The site of Oldham Road station today. (Author)

Miles Platting

John Hawkshaw established the principle engine shed and works at Miles Platting, a few miles outside of Manchester, where the stationary winding engine had been installed to haul trains up out of Manchester. Miles Platting depot came into operation in 1839, and the neighbouring workshops in December 1846. The engine shed was a timber roundhouse, 56 yards long and 21 yards wide. Behind it were built carriage and wagon workshops as well as locomotive repair facilities. The main building was brick, of three storeys, approximately 400 feet long and 75 feet wide. They were at a lower level than the engine shed, and approached by a steep incline. Additional wagon shops were built in 1847 (tenders were advertised in November 1846), giving the company the facilities to build its own locomotives and rolling stock. By 1851, two additional sheds had been provided alongside the original roundhouse: one five-road through shed, which connected with the roundhouse, and an eleven-road shed at Oldham Road, backing onto New Allen Street.

The buildings at Miles Platting were severely damaged by fire on 27 April 1873. Sixteen locomotives were destroyed within the workshops and a further seven in adjacent sidings. A great many carriages were also destroyed. This spurred on the Directors to provide new facilities sooner rather than later: a large twenty-four-road running shed was built at Newton Heath, coming into use in 1876, capable of holding 180 locomotives at a cost of £40,000. The build was 312 feet long, 328 feet wide, and covered some three acres of ground. New carriage and wagon works were built at Newton Heath and Miles Platting turned over solely to repairing locomotives until 1886, when the new Horwich Works were opened. Over 1,000 men were employed at Newton Heath and in 1879 a group of locomen founded the 'Newton Heath Cricket and Football Club', which today is Manchester United. Newton Heath Depot celebrated 125 years in 2001.

The great fire at Miles Platting Works. (Author's Collection)

James Fenton was appointed in 1840 as Superintendent and John Craven as Locomotive Foreman. Both were reprimanded by the Directors in 1843 for negligence, but it appears this did not change the work-ethic at Miles Platting as two years later the locomotive *Irk* exploded, killing the driver and fireman. The *Manchester Courier* (1 February 1845) reported:

> About six o'clock that morning, three engines and their tenders, the *Irk*, the *Trent*, and the *Mersey*, were lying in the shed ... Two men were at work at the west end, in the pit under the *Irk* engine, which had been undergoing a thorough repair ... and they were preparing it for the 7 ¼ a.m. train to Leeds. One of the men, named George Mills, the engineer and driver, was examining the connecting rods; the other, William Alcock, the fireman, was packing some of the glands at the other end of the engine. William Stone, the night inspector of engines, and Joseph Clark, the day inspector had just entered ... Stone remaining there [at the side of *Irk*]... Just at this moment ... exactly at six o'clock, an explosion took place with a large report, and a concussion which shook all the neighbourhood like an earthquake.... The *Irk* was thrown from its place ... projected with great force upwards ... turning over in its way. It ... passed quite over the *Trent* engine, carrying away its dome, chimney, whistle, &c., ... and ... through the roof ... it fell with its upper part downward. The explosion took place in the firebox ... The body of Mills, the engine-man, was found beneath the *Irk* engine ... Mr Craven upon calling the roll, found that two others were missing ... The body of Alcock, the fireman, was found crouched in a sitting position under the engine. That of William Stone ... was also found beneath the engine ... James Nelson was in the centre pit, beneath the *Mersey* engine at the same time, cleaning it, when the steam and burning coke were driven against him ... he was very extensively scalded. When found ... his clothes were on fire ... Another man, named John Wainwright, was injured by a slate from the roof falling on his head ... John Hall another man who was near at the time ... was slightly burned about the thighs.

Bury-type 0-4-0s were typical of Manchester & Leeds motive power of the 1840s. (Author's Collection)

At the inquest, William Fairbairn – the builder of *Irk* – found that neither of the safety valves were in working order, casting blame on the competency of the men working at Miles Platting and also Fenton (the Superintendent), who resigned on 20 February. The 3/8-inch-thick crown of the copper firebox had overheated and collapsed – suggesting water had dropped too low – and ruptured where it joined the back plate 'at that side nearest the fire-door' and was 'torn off entirely'. The force of the explosion had not only thrown *Irk* high into the air, but had 'considerably depressed the brick floor of the engine pit ... at least four inches'. A deodand of £500 was placed against the company. The explosion of *Irk* was reported far and wide; from Brighton to Thurso. As a result of this boiler explosion and others like it, William Fairbairn was inspired to establish the Manchester Steam Users Association in 1854 as the first body to inspect and insure steam boilers.

Opening Day

The first section of the line to be completed was that between Manchester and Littleborough, which was formally opened on 3 July 1839. A trial run had been made on 31 May, when Directors, shareholders, and friends boarded a special train of three carriages (two second- and one third-class) at the temporary station in Manchester to the summit. Due to the lack of any locomotive, the train was initially drawn by horses and set off at 10:50 a.m. Having reached Miles Platting, the party alighted and had to walk three-quarters of a mile to the next train, headed by the *Stephenson*. The train arrived at Rochdale at 12:35 p.m. where twenty minutes were spent taking on water, 'by means of a fire-engine, belonging to the Rochdale Police, pumping from a brook over which the railway passes'. The train finally arrived at the summit at 1:30 p.m., where an al-fresco luncheon was served, the party departing at 3 p.m., this time drawn by the *Lancaster*. The formal opening, however, was destined not to be quite so trouble free.

On 3 July two special trains of eleven coaches each (probably the company's entire stock), drawn by two locomotives carrying local worthies, Directors, shareholders, and persons of note from other railway companies. The first train was headed by *Stephenson* and *Kenyon*, and the second by *Stanley* and *Lancaster*. The first three had been built by R. Stephenson & Co., and were six-wheel 'large Samson' class, whilst the fourth – to the same design – was locally made by Sharp, Roberts & Co. of Manchester. In total the L&M would acquire twelve 'large Samson' types during 1839, supplied by four different builders. The carriages and engines were

> Decorated for the occasion with a number of small flags and banners, on most of which were inscribed some loyal sentiments as "Queen Victoria – God bless her!", "Long live the Queen", and "Peace and Concord."

As the first train climbed the steep (1: 130) gradient to Castleton, around 12:40 p.m., *Kenyon*'s water pump failed – upon dismantling it was found to be clogged with mud – and the fire had to be dropped. This left a single locomotive, *Stephenson*, to draw both the train and a 'dead' locomotive. In order to lighten the load, most of the 'gentlemen' alighted from the carriages, but luckily the second train headed by *Lancaster* arrived; both trains were coupled together and made slow progress to Littleborough and to the Summit Tunnel. A cold collation was held at Littleborough, where 500 guests sat down. The locomotives and carriages were sent back down the line to Rochdale to take on coke and water and where *Kenyon*'s water pump was cleared and repaired. Two trains were marshalled for the return journey; the first arriving in Manchester at 5:27 p.m. and the second an hour later. A timetable was published and issued the following day. The time of the train from Manchester to Littleborough was stated to be forty-five minutes. Manchester to Rochdale cost 3s first class, 2s second class, and 1s third class. Mills Hill to Littleborough was at the same rate. Between 4 July 1839 and 5 August, the M&L carried a staggering 57,820 passengers or '2,065 for every working day, not withstanding the late wet weather has, of course, been unfavourable to travelling'. The most passengers carried on a single day were 3,144.

The second section to be opened was that between Hebden Bridge to Mirfield in August 1840:

An experimental trip was made on part of the unopened line ... for the distance of sixteen miles ... At one o'clock PM a train of ten carriages drawn by eight horses decorated with evergreens and rosettes of the gayest description ... carrying nearly 100 individuals ... and accompanied by two bands of music which greatly livened the proceedings of the day.

(*Manchester Guardian* 15 August 1840)

The section between Normanton – where the M&L joined the North Midland – and Hebden Bridge was opened with 'great ceremony' on 5 October 1840. The 'Assistant Clerk-in-Charge' at Sowerby Bridge station was Bramwell Brontë – brother of the famous literary sisters – who was appointed in August 1840; he was promoted to 'Clerk-in-Charge' at Luddenden Foot a year later, but was dismissed in 1842 due to serious discrepancies being found in the accounts for which he could provide no explanation.

The first train, via Normanton to Hebden Bridge, departed from Leeds Hunslet Lane station at 7:53 a.m. Rolling stock and locomotives were provided by the North Midland. The number of carriages appeared to be inadequate, as many persons, despite having paid for the privilege, 'could not be accommodated':

The rush of those who had taken places to the carriages so alarming ... There being no room in the carriages, the adventurous travellers mounted the tops of the carriages, where already many persons were sitting as could be accommodated in that position; but those who could not sit stood upright, until the whole of the carriages were covered with a crowd of standers, and in that fearful position did they remain all the way to Hebden Bridge, stooping down as they passed under the tunnel and the numerous bridges, and then rising and cheering ... to the astonished spectators.

(*The Railway Times* 17 October 1840)

Not all newspapers were amused; the *Wakefield Journal* thought

We have seldom witnessed a more alarming scene. The train was proceeding at 20 mph and if a single individual had failed to stoop at the moment of passing under a bridge his brains must have been dashed out, and the fall of one person must have thrown many others off the carriages to their almost inevitable destruction. In the afternoon at Brighouse ... Captain Laws ... ordered out a waggon used for the conveyance of cattle in which those on the tops of the carriages were told they might be accommodated.

(Wakefield Journal 16 October 1840)

The *Railway Times* waxed lyrical about the scenery as the line climbed the Calder Valley, calling it 'increasingly beautiful and grand'. It continued by estimating that the final 'distance of nine miles, the final link in the chain' would be 'ready for opening in the first week of December, when the trains will pass uninterruptedly from Leeds to Manchester'. This final section was inspected by Lieutenant-Colonel Sir Frederic Smith RE on the behalf of the Board of Trade early in December, but he reported in his findings that the line was not quite ready to be opened and gain the sanction of the Board: fencing was incomplete, level-crossings were not gated, there were no police on the line and only the first-class carriages had sprung buffers, which, the Lieutenant-Colonel informed the Directors, were essential safety features for *all* classes of passenger. A second inspection was carried out in spring 1841 and the *Railway Times* of 6 March announced that the line had been pronounced fit to carry passengers and freight five days earlier. There was no formal opening, but *Herapath's Railway Journal* drew attention to two very unusual carriages used on the first train from Manchester to Leeds:

> Being of an entirely new construction, but somewhat different from each other. The body of one ... is 18 feet by 7, and is 6 feet 6 inches high. There is a compartment in the centre

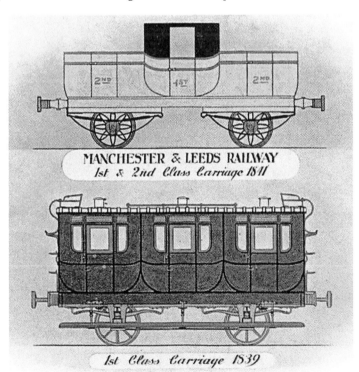

Examples of a 'Gondola' coach, and more conventional enclosed first-class vehicles used on the Manchester & Leeds. (Author's collection)

seven feet square ... fitted up with splendid mahogany sofas, lined with crimson plush ... and the top part above the sofa boxes comprised of plate glass with silk curtains. The two end compartments are open above; but a curtain of waterproof fabric can be drawn down at pleasure ... The other carriage, the Tourist, is similar in its general arrangements, but is fitted up differently. These carriages were made by Mr Mellings ... are adopted for summer travelling ... they are merely an experiment.

(*Herapath's Railway Journal* 13 March 1841)

Manchester was finally linked to Leeds by rail, against 'difficulties unprecedented in the annals of engineering'.

Manchester Victoria

Victoria Station, Manchester, is one of the best reminders of the early railways of Manchester and the pioneering spirit of the M&L, second only to the Summit Tunnel. The 'Hunts Bank' station, as Victoria was originally called, was one of the most controversial pieces of railway engineering in Manchester of the 1830s–40s. The railways had developed in a piecemeal fashion around Manchester, which – then as now – left the major terminal stations unconnected. The lack of a rail connection between Liverpool Road and Oldham Street not only constituted a lengthy and costly

Hunt's Bank Station, Manchester as depicted in 1845 by A. F. Tait. (National Railway Museum/ Science & Society Picture Library)

The interior of the original Hunt's Bank Station, with its single long platform. Note the two 'Gondola' coaches on the right. (National Railway Museum/Science & Society Picture Library)

delay for passengers and goods, but also the only missing link in a single line of railway communication from Liverpool to the Humber. At first, both the L&M and M&L were anxious to complete this connection; as early as November 1830, the L&M Directors were proposing such a link, despite the fact that the M&L would not open until 1836. Two years after opening, the M&L started negotiations to construct this 'missing link'. At first the L&M were amenable to forming a junction with the M&L in Salford at New Bailey Street, using an agreement with the MB&B (*Chapter 1*) to use part of their main line to make the connection. The Directors of the MB&B, however, upon seeing the cost declined, stating that they had no funds available. Thus, negotiations continued into the following year.

But it was not just the MB&B who began to get cold feet, so too the L&M. The L&M Directors instead proposed a junction – 'South Junction' – at Ordsall Lane to join with the Manchester & Birmingham at Store Street (*Chapter 4*), arguing that there was more traffic heading to Birmingham and thence London than east towards Leeds and Hull. By doing so they also hoped to compete with the Grand Junction – opened in 1837 – for Birmingham and London traffic. Naturally, the M&L were displeased with this change of tack and publicly condemned the L&M, having already commenced their own line from Miles Platting to Hunts Bank. This was completed by 1841 and arrangements were made so that passengers from Leeds could be booked through to Liverpool, with an Omnibus providing the link between the two stations. In the following year, with traffic on the M&L still not improving, the Directors of the L&M continued to decline to authorise the junction with the Leeds company.

Meanwhile, the M&B at Store Street had made alternative plans; to connect with the M&L at Hunts Bank via a stillborn project to tunnel under the city. The L&M, however, still preferred the 'South Junction' route and at a meeting of its Proprietors in March 1842 they discussed a proposal to link Liverpool Road, Store Street, and Hunts Bank via a loop line around the south side of Manchester. The M&L and MB&B, however, still favoured a northern junction via Salford linking Ordsall Lane to Hunts Bank; proposing the formation of the 'Northern Railway Company' to build and operate the line between them. Furthermore, the M&L threatened the L&M by proposing to build its own canal and transhipment warehouses alongside the Hunts Bank site and send freight for Liverpool onwards by water, rather than by the L&M. The *Manchester Guardian* weighed in, arguing that the two companies should unite in building the line linking the two stations; urging them to put aside petty 'local rivalries' and stressing the 'great important of this Hunts Bank Junction to the entire country'.

Finally, the L&M capitulated and in March and April 1842 thrashed out an agreement to build the linking line. An Act of Parliament was drafted and given Royal Assent on 30 July 1842, giving the L&M the power to build a junction from Ordsall Lane to Hunts Bank. Despite this apparent progress, the local press were growing weary of the squabbling; the *Manchester Guardian* accusing the L&M Directors of dithering and wasting too much time on a work of 'national importance'. Finally, contracts were signed and work was in progress by September 1842.

The extension was complete by spring 1844, on a site alongside the Workhouse and Pauper Burial Ground at Hunts Bank, despite fierce opposition from the Cathedral authorities. The new station at Hunts Bank opened on 4 May 1844 and the *Manchester Guardian* announced:

> There is now ... one continuous line of railway communication across the country from Hull to Liverpool, and the Irish Channel is thus brought into close neighbourhood with the German Ocean.

The same newspaper waxed lyrical about the new station, then the largest in the country:

> Arrival and Departure platforms for both companies ... covers a distance from Hunts Bank to Ducie bridge of 852 feet, with an average width of 130; having five main lines, and two are sidings for goods. In addition there are other sidings for goods; and the departure lines for the two railways are also sidings, on the south side of the other rails. To the length of 700 feet from Great Ducie street, the station will be covered by an iron roofing, erected in three compartments ...and an entire width of about 114 feet ... the largest extent of railway roofing in the Kingdom.
>
> The arrival and departure platforms are ... on the same side of the rails; viz. On the south side. The arrival platform for the Liverpool line is between the station-house and Ducie street; and to this there is a covered way for carriages; one half of the southern roof projecting over the arrival platform, so as to protect the passengers effectually from

Victoria Station *c.* 1890; the original 1844 building on the left. The other ranges date from the 1860s expansion. (Author's Collection)

Remains of the 1844 range in 2016, now used as staff accommodation. (Author)

the weather... The platforms are very large and convenient [The Liverpool platform] to a length of 184 feet, by 12 feet wide ... Towards Leeds the platform is continued for 120 feet ... the Length of the each departure platform is about 320 feet. The total length ... exceeds a thousand lineal feet.

(Manchester Guardian 19 August 1843).

A single storey 'station house' fronted the single platform, 'designed in the Roman Doric style', 266 feet long and 36 feet wide, built from York Stone quarried at Brighouse. The western wing of the building – which still survives in 2016 – was used by the L&M, whilst the eastern was occupied by the M&L. Linking them was a central block (still surviving), 'presenting a frontage 60 feet wide':

[This] freshment saloon is lighted with handsome circular headed windows, with stone pilasters and dressings, and surmounted by an elegant cornice, about the centre of which is a placed a large clock. To the right and left respectively are the booking-offices of the two companies, having entrances under a covered way, supported by brackets ... Internally, the large central refreshment room [measures] 40 feet 3 inches by 22 feet 2 inches. It contains also space for a bar &c. ... This room will have two entrance doors, both from the railway platform; one for the Liverpool and the other for Leeds passengers. This saloon is for the first- and second-class passengers only. A door at each end opens into the ladies' waiting rooms &c. This saloon itself will be the gentlemen's waiting room.

(Manchester Guardian 19 August 1843).

The 1844 'Freshment Saloon' – the second storey was added in the 1860s. (Author)

Third-class – and later Parliamentary Class – passengers could not be admitted to this waiting room, instead the 'refreshment room ... [with] a bar and every convenience and accommodation suitable for that class of passenger' was in the basement, along with the kitchens and 'rooms for porters', and other station functionaries.

Locomotives on the M&L did not work into Victoria – the extension from Miles Platting was worked as an inclined plane, and trains were hauled up and lowered down by two winding engines at the top of the bank:

> The junction line descends from the main line, by a steep inclined plane, the inclination of the first part of which is 1 in 49, and of the remainder 1 in 60. This plane is worked by stationary engines and endless ropes, directions being conveyed to from end to end by an electric telegraph; and from it's lower extremity to the Hunt's Bank, or, as it is now called the Victoria Station, is a rising gradient of 1 in 132, which is ascended by the impetus obtained in descending the inclined plane, and is descended by trains going to Leeds by gravity alone.
>
> (*The British Almanac*, 1845)

The winding engines remained in use only for a few years, as locomotives developed to be able to scale the bank. Another preclusion to through-running was that the M&L was

The original 1844 bridge spanning Ducie Street; Chetham's School of Music can be seen through the arch. (Author)

laid to a gauge of 4 feet 9 inches – half an inch wider than the L&M. By the end of 1844 the L&M were selling through-tickets from Liverpool to Leeds (onwards travel from Leeds by the Leeds & Selby), but after about six months this break in the journey was leading to numerous complaints from passengers. The Board of the L&M approached the M&L as to whether 'the railway was in a safe state as to the *Gauge* of their rails to admit the Liverpool Carriages'.

Most of the 1840s station was swept away in 1909 when Victoria was re-modelled under William Dawes, providing some seventeen platforms and an Edwardian façade set at ninety degrees to that of 1844. It was disfigured by the construction of the Arena over the former through-platforms – the site of the original 1844 station – between 1992 and 1996. In August 2010 Network Rail announced a multi-million pound refurbishment programme at Victoria, including a completely new roof, which alone cost £17 million. Work commenced in autumn 2013 and completed in August 2015, creating a bright, airy, and watertight station concourse.

The imposing Edwardian façade of Victoria, designed by William Dawes and completed in 1909. (Author)

The scale of the 1909 building – 146 metres long – is readily apparent. (Author)

The elegant, tiled Edwardian interior of Victoria in 1925. (Author's Collection)

The same scene nearly a century later, following its multi-million pound facelift. (Author)

W. H. Smith's bookstore in 1925. (Author's Collection)

The beautifully restored bookstall now houses the information office. (Author)

An early colourised postcard of Victoria, issued by the Lancashire & Yorkshire Railway, *c.* 1910.

CHAPTER 4

The Manchester & Birmingham Railway (1842)

The Manchester & Birmingham (M&B) was born out of rivalry between the businessmen of Manchester and Liverpool, who not only resented the power of the 'Liverpool Party' in the national railway scene, but with the circuitous route between Manchester and Birmingham via the Grand Junction Railway (GJR). To complicate matters, the M&B grew out of two rival schemes from Manchester to Birmingham – a destination the M&B never reached.

Coat of Arms of the Manchester & Birmingham Railway, carried on the sole surviving piece of rolling stock. (Author/MSI Manchester)

The Manchester & Cheshire Junction Railway

The first scheme to link Manchester to Birmingham via a direct route was the Manchester & Cheshire Junction (M&CJ), which proposed in 1835 – two years before the opening of the GJR – to build a line from Manchester via Stockport and Wilmslow to Crewe, where it would connect with the GJR; thus cutting off a considerable detour. Not only was the M&CJ to connect with the GJR but also with a proposed line to Chester, and, ultimately, to North Wales and Holyhead for the Irish mail traffic. The engineer was John Urpeth Rastrick. The *Chester Chronicle* (20 November 1830) noted:

> The undertaking stands prominently forward, not only for the *obvious necessity* of such a mode of internal communication as it will supply between Manchester and the neighbouring populous manufacturing districts in Cheshire, and as *the most direct route* from that great emporium of trade and manufacturers to the metropolis, but [also] from the energy and despatch with which the project was conceived and put into operation ...

The Manchester & Birmingham Railway and its rivals. (Andy Mason)

A provisional committee was formed in summer 1835, chaired by Robert Barbour Esq., a wealthy Manchester textile merchant and banker, who founded Robert Barbour & Brother in 1816 and was a proprietor of the Manchester & Liverpool District Bank founded in 1829, which, unsurprisingly, was the bank of the M&CJ. The Deputy Chairman was John Brooks Esq., a wealthy calico printer trading as 'Butterworth & Brooks' of Manchester. Brooks was a keen advocate of free trade and vocal opponent of the Corn Laws. The Secretary was Ralph Ellis Jnr, a Manchester solicitor. The committee consisted of the Borough reeves of Manchester and Salford, the Mayors of Macclesfield and Congleton and various Manchester worthies. The provisional committee issued its *Prospectus* in November 1835, expressing their dissatisfaction with existing routes south from Manchester:

> The London and Birmingham and Grand Junction Railways, will, when completed, form a direct communication between the Metropolis and Liverpool – not so, however, with Manchester! That place, and the vastly important district of which it is the centre, will not, according to existing arrangements, have any direct Railway communication with London ... The desirable results it is proposed to accomplish and place Manchester in the position which Liverpool, by means of the railways, now in course of completion, will be, viz.:-
>
> To give it a direct railway communication with the Metropolis;
>
> To save the parties travelling to Manchester to London an utterly useless circuit of seventeen miles;
>
> To give Stockport, Macclesfield, and Congleton, a Direct Railway to Manchester, and an equally direct railway communication with London ...
>
> The advantages of the undertaking are too apparent to require more than cursory glance. The intercourse which Manchester maintains with London, Birmingham, Bristol, and other towns in the south and west of England, as well as that for shorter distances – such as Stockport, Macclesfield, and Congleton – is already greater than any other district of England.

The M&CJ received considerable local support; of the shareholders 282 were residents of Manchester, the remainder living within 20 miles of that town. There was also considerable support from communities near Birmingham; 'A numerous and Highly Respectable meeting of Iron Masters and owners of property in the vicinity of Wolverhampton' was held in April 1836, and a committee was formed in support of the proposed railway, which issued four resolutions giving their backing to the scheme. The towns of Macclesfield and Congleton also lent their support to the new railway. Backing also came from the Chester & Crewe Railway and the Wolverhampton & Worcester Railway Company.

The Manchester South Union Railway

The second proposal was far more ambitious and known as the Manchester South Union (MSU). It planned a railway from Manchester through Macclesfield and the Potteries, eventually joining the London & Birmingham Railway at Rugby. The Chairman of the MSU was the wealthy Liverpool banker and slave-owner John Moss, who had been the Deputy Chairman of the Liverpool & Manchester and was also Chairman of the GJR. The MSU, however, was initially condemned by both George Stephenson and Joseph Locke (engineer of the GJR and by then estranged from Stephenson), and also John Rastrick. Stephenson wrote:

> My first survey commenced at Manchester, having in view the towns of Macclesfield, Congleton, the neighbourhood of the Potteries; I found the country pretty favourable until reaching Macclesfield, *when it rises to at least 150 feet above the summit level ... a circumstance alone which is so objectionable, that I cannot recommend it for a main line.*

Locke added that the 'line through Macclesfield is a bad one' and, in order to maintain workable gradients, would have required considerable tunnelling or a major detour. He recommended instead the route proposed by the M&CJ. Rastrick believed that the ridge of hills between Cheshire and the Potteries presented a considerable obstacle. Stephenson, however, after carrying out a second survey of the route, came out in favour of the proposed line:

> From Manchester the Line went direct to Stockport, and form Stockport to Pointon, at an ascent of sixteen feet in the mile: from thence to Macclesfield, at part eighteen feet, and part twenty feet in the mile ascent: from thence by Dane's Moss to Congleton at sixteen feet ascent: and from Congleton to Harecastle, on a dead level, or nearly so ... After passing Harecastle it goes through the Potteries in a most advantageous manner: from the Potteries to Stone, on favourable ground, no part above fourteen feet in the mile: from thence it goes to the Birmingham and Derby Line.

There was considerable rivalry between the two schemes and their promoters; the MSU going so far as to print derogatory handbills and attempting to disrupt meetings of the M&CJ. There was also friction between the MSU and GJR, especially as the former were in negotiations for amalgamation with the Derby & Birmingham Railway Company. Whilst the GJR were not 'opposed to their application for shortening their line to London', if the line had not been 'made within a reasonable time ... the South Union shall be at liberty to pursue their original plan'. The MSU also proposed a line 'along the Trent' from Tamworth to Rugby to join the Birmingham & Derby. Ultimately, the MSU informed the GJR that:

> The South Union committee deeply regret that your committee should not have concurred in their opinion that Manchester and London, and to the intermediate populous districts, are of insufficient importance to warrant the formation of the best independent railway communication of which the country will admit, regardless of any conflicting interests.
>
> (*Liverpool Mail* 24 November 1836)

Passing through Parliament

The cost of the M&CJ was estimated at £546,000, and the first Bill passed through the Commons on 18 August 1836 and came before the Lords two days later. In the Commons it had been supported by no fewer than twenty-one Members for Lancashire, but in the Lords it was fiercely opposed by Mr Wilbraham Egerton of Tatton Park – a major landowner, who would be a thorn in the side of several railway projects during the 1830s. Given that the

MSU and M&CJ provided nearly parallel routes, the Bill was put to arbitration in the Lords. The Bill was modified by the Lords who,

> After a careful examination of the subject, decided that the Line from Manchester to Crewe in substance is expedient, we recommend that the Stockport be now included in such line, which would be used by both the Manchester and Cheshire, and also by the South Union Railways; and that the level shall be as such as may be applicable to the South Union Railway.

The MSU had scored the first victory but the M&CJ was not finished yet: a meeting of shareholders and proprietors met at the Albion Hotel, Manchester, 1 September 1836, along with deputations from Macclesfield and Congleton. The shareholders resolved to 'go again to Parliament next session for an Act'. A deputation headed by John Brooks met with the Stockport Town Council to garner their support; the Stockport Council expressing 'no tie to either party' and wished to have 'the best line', but when pushed to the point found 'the proposals of the Cheshire Junction Committee very reasonable'. The *Manchester Courier*, a keen supporter of the M&CJ, opined that the 'Cheshire Junction ... [is] the more rational scheme both with reference to the public generally, and in a pecuniary point of view to the shareholders'. It noted somewhat ironically that the two rival camps represented town versus country, and that their squabbling would mean that neither proposed railway was built:

> Who are the South Unionists? They were composed of Manchester, Stockport, Macclesfield, and Congleton; and what did the Cheshire Junction consist of? Of Manchester men only. The majority of the South Union Committee where not Manchester men [but rather] the people of Stockport, Macclesfield and Congleton.

The *Courier* also opined that whilst the M&CJ had the shorter and flattest route, because it passed through a largely agricultural area, it would never have the same amount of traffic as the MSU which 'passed through many large towns' and, in the end, this would be deciding factor over which railway would be built.

In the meantime, the MSU, headed by John Moss, approached the M&CJ regarding amalgamation of the two concerns and for 'making a common line to or near Stafford.' As the 'overture seemed a feasible one', both companies appointed deputations to thrash out the exact details. The only major stumbling block was

> Whether the Line should pass through Congleton, or by the way of Macclesfield and Leek. This question, the Sub-committee found it impossible to arrange ... The correspondence terminated unsuccessfully, in consequence of an almost entire alteration of the plan by the South Union Company, and of their choosing to require a new basis of negotiation.

The M&CJ committee presented a new *Prospectus* in December 1836, with a revised route which now included Stockport and Congleton with a proposed junction with the GJR at Rugeley.

Both schemes went before Parliament during 1837 and a compromise was reached. One Captain Alderson recommended that the proposed route between Alderly to Congleton and

Harecastle be approved, but that the line then follow the MSU to Chebsey where it would join the GJR. By an Act of 30 June 1837, both rival undertakings were incorporated as the Manchester & Birmingham Railway (M&B), with branches from Alderley to Crewe, and from Stockport to Macclesfield (the latter originally proposed by the MSU).

The Manchester & Birmingham Railway

The first general meeting of the company was held in Manchester at the York Hotel, on Monday 30 July 1837, and the first business was to appoint Directors and unite the two factions. Arbitration and conciliation between the two companies had been taking place since December 1836. Even so, the first meeting was still tense, with the 'South Unionists' still proposing to 'take the line over the hills' to the south, whilst the 'Cheshire Junctionists' were intent on 'abandoning their present line, and go only to Crewe'. Amongst the shareholders were Robert and Thomas Ashton – Unitarian mill owners of Hyde – and the Rev. William Gaskell; Thomas would be elected Chairman in 1839. The Ashtons were also major shareholders in the Sheffield, Ashton-under-Lyne and Manchester Railway, which was intext on building a mainline through the Pennines to Sheffield, which opened via the famous Woodhead Tunnels in 1845. Other shareholders included John Bulkeley Johnson Esq. – the Mayor of Congleton – and Watkin Lees Esq. – a wealthy Cotton Spinner of Dukinfield.

George Watson Buck was appointed as Engineer. He was a Quaker, and had been educated at the Friends' School, Ackworth. He had served as Engineer to the Montgomeryshire Canal (1819) and had been part of Robert Stephenson's team building the London & Birmingham Railway. Construction began between Manchester and Stockport on 14 August 1838.

Opening the Line

The first section of the line to be built and opened was that from Manchester to Stockport; the line left Store Street on a brick viaduct at Chancery Lane and then ran more or less parallel with Hyde Road on a viaduct of fifty-two arches, each of 36 feet span; only six had been completed by September 1839. Hyde Road was crossed by an iron skew bridge, similar to that crossing Fairfield Street in Manchester. From Hyde Road the line ran on an embankment and thence through a cutting at Heaton Norris. From here it ran on a second embankment to the northern abutment of the Stockport Viaduct. The bridge carrying the railway over Stockport Road was 'from the patterns made for the Hyde Road Bridge'. This bridge was demolished in 1957 and replaced with a concrete structure.

Work commenced on the Stockport Viaduct on 10 March 1839. By September 1839 George Buck was able to report that

> The north abutment is built to the level of the cornice. Three arches are turned and backed; the fourth is nearly so; the centring for the fifth is being fixed; the sixth and seventh piers are built, and the imposts are upon them ready for centring; the base of the eighth pie is complete, and that of the ninth is just begun.

The twenty-seven-arch viaduct took twenty-one months to build, using 11 million bricks at a cost of £70,000. It was completed on December 21 1840, when a ceremony marked the laying of the final stone. The first train to cross Stockport Viaduct did so on 30 July 1841, drawing a specially decorated train of twelve carriages.

The iron skew bridge carrying the Manchester & Birmingham line over Fairfield Street, Manchester. (Author's Collection)

A testimony to the ambition of the Manchester & Birmingham Railway: the twenty-seven-arch Stockport Viaduct. (Author)

The Congleton Viaduct, crossing the Dane, was begun in mid-September 1839 when some 'Eight million of bricks' had been made for its construction. Captain Edward John Cleather, of Ardwick House, Manchester, who had previously served in the Royal Staff Corps, was appointed general manager of the line under the title of 'Outdoor Superintendent and Secretary'.

The first train from Manchester to Stockport ran on 4 June 1840 from the temporary station in Travis Street to a temporary station at Warren Street in Stockport. First-class tickets cost 1s 6d; second-class 1s; and third-class 6d. There were thirteen trains each day. Because there were run-round facilities but no turn-table at Stockport, locomotives ran from Manchester travelling smoke-box first, but on the return journey had to run tender-first. The enterprising folk of Gorton established a 'Fly Boat' along the Stockport Branch Canal from Gorton to Stockport, but this was discontinued with the opening of the line in full two years later.

The track was laid on stone blocks à la Stephenson, using 'T' section malleable iron rails weighing 68 lbs per yard in 15-foot lengths, laid at the gauge of 4 feet 9 inches. 'Switches and attached telegraph' were supplied by Messrs. Ellis and Notton, the patentees, and consisted of

A ponderous piece or plate of iron, with the rails and flanges requisite upon its surface ... the direction ...for which the switch is set ... is made manifest, by a patent indicator, or signal plate, connected with the switch, which consists ... of an upright rod of iron, surmounted by a large iron disc ... painted so as to be seen at a considerable distance. When the switches are set for the siding, the disc faces up the road, and is a very conspicuous warning ... If ... the switches are set for the mainline, only the edge of the disc ... is presented, indicating all is right.

(*Manchester Times* 6 June 1840)

A typical Sharp, Stewart 2-2-2 well tank as used by the Manchester & Birmingham. (Author's Collection)

In total twenty-two 2-2-2 tank locomotives were supplied by Messrs Sharp, Roberts & Co. between 1840 and 1842. An additional two were purchased second-hand from Messrs. Fairbairn. Four of the Sharp, Roberts locomotives were sold to the South Eastern Railway.

The M&B had some ninety carriages; forty-eight First-class, twenty-four Second-class and twenty-four Third class. In addition were freight wagons. In January 1845 the company were advertising for tenders for

One Pleasure Carriage, Four Milk Trucks, and FIFTY Box Waggons, with drawing- and buffer springs.

The passenger carriages were painted dark blue, and the Firsts and Seconds were lined out in gilt, red and black and 'upon the centre panel of each First-class carriage are the arms of the Manchester & Birmingham Railway.' The number of each carriage was painted 'near the bottom at each end'. First-class carriages were fully enclosed, with three compartments seating six persons each. Second-class were similar, but had four compartments seating eight; the vehicles were 'open through [i.e. no internal partitions] ... the seats not cushioned

The lovingly restored Manchester & Birmingham first-class coach at MOSI, Manchester. (Author/ MSI Manchester)

The luxurious – if claustrophobic – interior of the coach. (Lauren Jaye Gradwell, 2016)

or divided.' The compartment doors of the Seconds were lettered A, B, C or D. The Third-class carriages were 'simple open boxes' similar to those on the M&L, which were estimated to carry 'forty or fifty persons each.'

Manchester London Road

Manchester's fourth railway station was opened on a temporary site in Travis Street in May 1840 when the line to Stockport was opened. The *Manchester Courier* (6 June 1840) described the temporary station as being 'convenient' and

> Formed under three of the arches... the space obtained will be amply sufficient for the purposes of the company... Entering the station by a door on the side of the arches next Fairfield-street, the passengers ascend to the line by means of a temporary wooden staircase, which is erected outside the arches, and enclosed; and walking a few yards forward, they find the carriages drawn up, ready for their reception.

The new station at Store Street in Manchester was considered an improvement on that at Liverpool Road because it was 'extremely central, and at much less distance from the principal inns and public buildings'. A major problem faced by the M&B was that their initial Act forbade the company from crossing Store Street, or 'carrying it over any street at

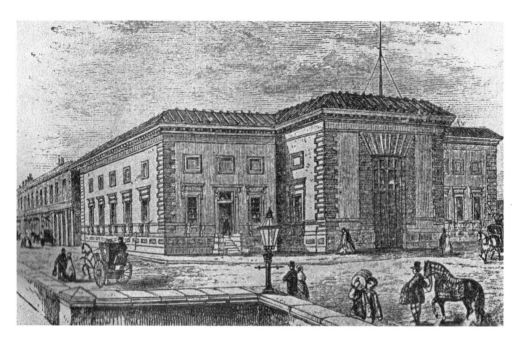

A contemporary depiction of Store Street Station, latterly London Road. (Author's Collection)

Another contemporary image: this time of the colossal iron viaduct supporting London Road Station – and still supporting Manchester Piccadilly to this day. (Author)

a greater width than sixty feet'. This produced a very cramped station, 'within very narrow limits ... [and] very inconvenient approaches'. In order to remedy this, the company spent a whopping £40,000 for a new Act in 1839, which gave them powers to 'enlarge the station to a length of 670 feet and a breadth of 180 feet', as well as being able to bridge Store Street.

The expansion of the site necessitated the demolition of the old 'London Road Inn' and closure of the London Road Market and various coal wharfs adjoining the canal.

One of the most admired engineering aspects of the line into Manchester was the iron skew bridge over Fairfield Street, set at an angle of 24.5 degrees; its span was 128 feet 9 inches but 'the square span of the street is not more than 48 feet'. The cast-iron parapets bore shields bearing the arms of the M&B and the inscription 'Manchester and Birmingham Railway 1839'. When this bridge was dismantled the decorative panels were recovered and are now part of the National Collection.

In 1839 the M&B had granted the fledgling Sheffield, Ashton-under-Lyne & Manchester Railway (SA&M) running rights into its proposed Store Street terminal. The M&B also 'contracted to sell ... a certain plot of land in Store-Street, for the purpose of a Good's Station' to the SA&M. If, however, the SA&M were to use that land for a passenger station, they had to provide a separate approach at their own cost. Running rights into the new station via a junction at Ardwick were renewed in March 1841 but SA&M were now also obliged to pay for the upkeep of the track and viaduct from Chancery Lane Junction to Store Street; the M&B were also empowered to charge 2d per passenger and 3d per ton of freight passing over the line into the station. The Directors Meeting reported in February 1842 that the new joint station on Store Street was rapidly approaching completion.

Store Street was opened with little fanfare on Tuesday 10 May 1842. It was officially renamed 'London Road' in 1847, although newspapers had been referring to it as such from opening, so perhaps the name change brought it into line with popular usage. The *Manchester Courier* (12 May 1842) described the new building:

> Erected on a viaduct of sixteen arches, 238 feet long, 34 feet span, rising to the height of 30 feet above London-Road. These arches are fitted up as warehouses for the parties who have arranged with the company for the conveyance of merchandize along the line. The approach to the passenger station is by an incline from Ducie-Street. Facing the approach, at the top of the incline, is a beautiful stone building, in the Italian style of architecture, which forms the prominent feature of the station ... Turning to the left, the visitor approaches a range of buildings 500 feet long, containing the booking offices, waiting rooms, parcels offices, &c., which are particularly spacious and convenient; over these, and connected by a corridor extending the whole length, are the proprietor's meeting rooms, directors' and treasurer's rooms, manager's and engineer's rooms, and the offices for the various clerks of the company.

The new station had only two platforms – arrival and departure:

> Passing through the booking offices, he will arrive on a platform for passengers on departure. This is 500 feet in length, and 12 feet wide, the platform floor being laid with asphalt: this platform, together with the two departure lines of rails, is covered with a light iron roof, 480 feet long, and 34 feet span. On the opposite side of the station is the platform for the arrival lines, 312 feet long and 12 feet wide, beyond which again is a spacious area for carriages waiting the arrival of passengers. This is paved with wooden blocks ... between the platform are six lines of rails connected with three rows

The Italianate façade of London Road Station, built in 1865. Sadly, it was demolished ninety-five years later and replaced by an inelegant concrete box. (Author's Collection)

An early colour postcard depicting the approach to London Road, in the age of electric trams and large hats. (Author's Collection)

Manchester Piccadilly in summer 2016. (Author)

of turntables; four of these lines are connected with a turntable, thirty feet in diameter, so arranged as to turn an engine and tender at once ... this part of the station is covered with an iron roof, 212 feet long, in two spans of 52 feet 6 inches, and 34 respectively.

The iron roof was supplied by Messrs. Bramah, Fox & Co. of Birmingham and was 'justly admired'. Goods facilities were provided by a massive brick-built warehouse on the north eastern side of the site. It was built by George Clarke Pauling of Manchester in just under twelve months (work commenced 12 June 1841), using 'twenty three million bricks ... and 800 tons of cast iron'. The *Manchester Guardian* expressed considerable doubt over the working of the joint station, especially due to narrow bottle-neck of the station approach:

> Some caution will be requisite hereto prevent two trains... coming into contact at this point. This, of course, may be done by arranging the times, or keeping the rails separate... at present the proper precaution seems to be to stand a watchman there to keep a look-out on both lines, and see that when a train is arriving on one line, there is no train arriving on the other, or if there be, to make the signal to one of them to slacken speed.
>
> (*Manchester Guardian* 20 November 1841)

The cramped station approach was widened through an Act of 22 July 1848, which also authorised construction of a viaduct over Sheffield Street linking the railway to newly built warehouses. By the early 1850s the buildings were considered 'dingy' and 'disgraceful.'

The original M&B station was demolished in 1861, which in turn was replaced less than a century later by a rather basic concrete box when the station was modernised and renamed Manchester Piccadilly. The present Piccadilly station was opened in 2002 in time for the Commonwealth Games, which Manchester hosted in that year.

Fighting for existence

In 1841, Captain Mark Huish was appointed Secretary and General Manager of the GJR. Born in Nottingham of good Dissenting (later Unitarian) stock, he had been denied a commission in the British Army due to his religious beliefs and was therefore commissioned in the forces of the Honourable East India Company, where he gained considerable administrative experience. Always ambitious, he had a vision for a single railway company between London and the North, with himself at the head of it. With the appointment of Huish, the relationship with the GJR deteriorated even further, especially as the opening of the M&B grew closer. The original agreement between the M&B and the GJR granted running powers over GJR metals through to Birmingham. By 1842, however, the GJR had 'set its face against MBR trains running to Birmingham in any circumstance'. Not only had it dissuaded the M&B from building its extension to Rugby to join the London & Birmingham Railway, it had reneged on its running-rights agreement; an agreement that had probably been extracted so long as the M&B abandoned its extension. The GJR, by astute political manoeuvring, had nullified the threat of the more direct route from Manchester to Birmingham offered by the M&B, and had deprived it not only of Birmingham and London traffic, but that for Chester and North Wales – thence Ireland – too. The M&B, therefore, opened only as far as Sandbach on 10 May 1842.

Such was the level of hostility between the two companies that the M&B postponed opening to Crewe for three months; even then its solitary platform was separate from, and outside, the GJR station. The GJR in a final, dramatic *coup*, then declared that it would be unsafe for M&B trains to use GJR metals as it 'had recently made a rule ... that the time interval between passenger trains ... must be no less than 30 minutes'. Whilst the GJR board insisted this was for 'public safety' – and indeed they did manage to get public opinion on their side – it effectively meant that the M&B was halted at Crewe. Eventually, the Board of Trade had to intervene in the negotiations. The M&B, supported by HM Inspector of Railways, argued that a five-minute interval between passenger trains departing 'principal stations' was safe and that the GJR suggesting a thirty-minute interval was unnecessary. At length, the M&B capitulated to the GJR, who by this point had got public opinion on their side, no matter what the Board of Trade might say. The GJR undertook to work M&B trains from Crewe to Birmingham for 70 per cent of the receipts for a period of three years. Thereafter M&B were allowed to work its own trains *back* from Birmingham, but not *to*.

In order to break the monopoly of the London & Birmingham on traffic to the metropolis, several prominent Manchester businessmen established the 'London & Manchester Direct Independent Railway'. It was proposed to put the Bill before Parliament in June 1845, with an anticipated cost of £3 million. The scheme was wound-up in 1849 after the shareholders discovered that the 'Directors had entered into some arrangements for amalgamation with a competing line'.

The next battle faced by the M&B was over the right to carry the Royal Mail. The GJR had, from 1837, been carrying the mail for Liverpool and Manchester, but in September 1842, Manchester Town Council proposed that mail from Manchester be sent south via the M&B, thus avoiding the delay and expense of the L&M and GJR. A petition was sent from Manchester to the Postmaster General – the Rt Hon Viscount Lowther – signed by the 'great and good' and dated 7 September 1842. Unsurprisingly, this was opposed by the GJR.

Two years later the issue was raised in the House by Mr Thomas Milner Gibson, MP for Manchester. The Prime Minister, Sir Robert Peel, noted 'the only objection ... was the fear of expense to the public by the terms demanded by the railways'. In his opinion, 'the Railway Companies could not better recommend themselves to public favour, than by shewing a disposition to facilitate intercourse by letter'. Sadly, 'after some further discourse, Mr M. Gibson withdrew his motion'. The GJR had scored another victory.

The M&B also 'found itself at loggerheads with the [Manchester &] Leeds Company', as, contrary to an earlier agreement, the M&L was sending its London traffic via Normanton and thence the North Midland Railway rather than via the M&B. Despite the protests of the M&B, the M&L complained that the rates of the M&B were 'excessive' and that 'it had no powers to compel carriers to transfer their goods to the more direct route'. Once again, it appears that the hand of the GJR was at work; the fact of the matter seems to have been that the GJR increased its own rates to compensate for the loss of Manchester traffic to the M&B, so in turn the M&B had to raise its rates to cover the increase in charges between Crewe and Birmingham, inflicted upon it by the GJR.

THE RAILWAY STATION, CREWE.

Crewe Railway Station, c. 1840, where Manchester & Birmingham Railway trains terminated, somewhat short of their intended destination. (Author's Collection)

Enter George Hudson

Hudson, the erstwhile 'Railway King', together with his deputy, Mr David Waddington, managed to get themselves elected to a committee of shareholders of the M&B in September 1842. The committee had been appointed in the light of the various disputes with neighbouring railways to 'discuss future policy with the directors'. By the end of the year, Hudson and Waddington had managed to get themselves elected as Directors – Waddington eventually rising to be Deputy Chairman to Thomas Ashton. In March 1843 the M&B Directors 'recommend a rather generous dividend', which resulted in several of the shareholders suggesting that the Board must have been paying dividends out of the capital account – something that, it later transpired, was a typical Hudson trick.

It was whilst Hudson was a Director that the M&B started to make overtures together with the Midland Railway about leasing the SA&M, as well as with the M&L regarding building a branch line from Store Street to Victoria. The M&B were also able to extract themselves from paying £50 per week compensation money to the latter concern 'for lost London traffic'. This latter payment was discontinued in 1843, 'making an important annual saving', and the Directors found that their 'traffic had not suffered by it'. It was also hoped that the GJR would allow the M&B to affect 'means of communication with Chester and North Wales' via the Crewe & Chester. The idea of building the branch to

MR. G. HUDSON, M.P.—"THE RAILWAY KING."

George Hudson, MP (1800–1871) 'The Railway King' seen at the height of his powers. (Author's Collection)

Macclesfield was also raised; finally authorised in 1844 as a revised, cheaper plan, running from Cheadle and passing close to Poynton collieries before terminating on the north side of Macclesfield at Beech Bridge. On the one hand, the Macclesfield Branch would increase traffic – and therefore revenue – on the line, but, on the other, under the terms of the Act of Incorporation, dividends could not be paid at more than 5 per cent until the Macclesfield line had been opened.

Questions of how the branch was to be funded was raised by the shareholders. David Waddington, who had taken the chair in absence of Ashton, stated that surplus funds would be used, as well as the money saved by not paying the M&L £50 per week, but this did not soothe all of the shareholders. Questions were raised over the £2,000 'annual allowance' of the Directors; many shareholders contending it was excessive and recommending it be reduced to £400. Branches were also proposed to Altrincham (to counter the Manchester South Junction & Altrincham Railway) and to Buxton, in order to oppose the proposed Manchester, Buxton, Matlock & Midland Junction Railway which would have run from the Midland Railway to the M&B at Cheadle. A new station was opened at Stockport Edgeley (renamed Heaton Norris) and at Longsight – where the Locomotive and Carriage Depot was located – in May 1843. A brick-built polygonal 'Roundhouse' engine shed, called 'The Polygon', was constructed – 48-yards (44 metres) in diameter and with a conical roof 40 feet high (12 metres), supported on massive cast-iron columns. Internally there were twelve roads, each with their own ash- and inspection pit, surrounding a central turntable. In addition were workshops, coke stores, and mess rooms. Sadly, it was in 'The Polygon' that five men – Edward Hefron (26), the driver; Thomas Gresty (32); James Snowdon (23); James Moore (36); and William Black (26) – were killed when the boiler of LNWR

A LNWR postcard of Macclesfield town and (latterly) LNWR station, built by the Manchester & Birmingham during Hudson's chairmanship. (Author's Collection)

locomotive No. 1 exploded early in the morning of 8 March 1853. The locomotive was blown through the roof of the shed – a third of which came crashing down – and landed nearly thirty yards away. A further thirteen men who had been stood around the engine warming themselves were seriously wounded. The coroner's inquest noted that No. 1, 'the oldest locomotive' – a 2-2-2 built by Sharp, Roberts & Co. of Manchester – had been under repair for two months and was considered too worn-out for passenger work, but was being repaired for 'light and Pilot-Engine in the Standedge Tunnel'. The coroner noted a poor level of safety-consciousness at Longsight and that Hefron had 'screwed down the safety-valve', which lead to a build-up of excess pressure resulting in the explosion. The case was turned over to HM Inspector of Railways, and both William Fairbairn and Richard Roberts presented reports on the condition of the boiler. Captain Wynne, on behalf of the Railway Inspectorate, rejected the idea that the safety valves had been tampered with. He found that the 13-year-old boiler was 'greatly reduced in thickness' and 'much honeycombed'. He blamed a poor safety culture and the neglected state of the engine which, because of its age and because it was a shunting engine, had not been getting proper maintenance and attention. Longsight Depot celebrated its 175th anniversary in 2017.

The M&B also made successful attempts to stimulate the tourist trade by popularising excursions to beauty spots such as Alderley Edge, where in June 1843 3,000 excursionists were carried on a single day. *The Railway Times* noted the train consisted of sixty-two carriages, was a quarter of a mile in length, and drawn by two engines! A hotel was later built there by the Company. The M&B also organised a more genteel 'Special Train for the Whitsun Holidays, to London and Back' for middle-class passengers that same summer. Some 500 persons were carried in sixteen carriages, which departed London Road at 8 a.m. and arrived at Euston Square at 7 p.m. The excursionists were put up in the Hotel at Euston and spent Whitsun in London.

Hudson resigned from the M&B in May 1845 and in September the shareholders met to consider amalgamation with the London & Birmingham, and the two systems began working 'as one' in January 1846.

CONCLUSION

Consolidation and Amalgamation

By 1845 the railways of Manchester had matured into a form that is recognisable today and that remained static for the next twenty-five or so years, until the opening of Central and Exchange. Indeed, with the closure of those two stations and concentration of services at Victoria, Piccadilly and the re-modelling of Salford Central, the wheel has turned full circle, with the emphasis once again on Manchester's oldest stations. There was, however, one major difficulty that still persists today; all of these stations were on the periphery of the city and there was no through-running, something the Ordsall Chord is hoping to address.

The SA&M had originally intended to join up with the L&M in an end-on junction at Liverpool Road. Sadly, this did not come to fruition due to the constant feuding and jockeying for position by all the rival companies in Manchester. As we have seen, the L&M, despite its initial enthusiasm for linking up with the M&L at Victoria, was not necessarily in favour of such a link until forced to do so; on the one hand believing there was insufficient traffic to merit it, and then that such a link would take traffic away from its own line. It was only the threat of the M&L building a canal basin alongside Victoria for onward shipping of traffic to Liverpool that finally spurred the reluctant L&M into action. The L&M, however, remained in favour of through-running via the SA&M and M&B at Store Street to gain access to the lucrative industrial centres of Sheffield and Birmingham, proposing a South Junction Railway as early as 1838. This link eventually appeared as the Manchester South Junction Railway, was jointly owned by the SA&M and M&B, and was conceived of by Joseph Locke of the M&B as 'a species of bridge to provide cross-town communication'. The line was carried entirely on a brick viaduct. An Act was obtained in 1845 and contracts let at the end of the same year to David Bellhouse Jr of Manchester. Always short of money – some 64 per cent of the costs was for land and compensation payments – it finally opened on 1 August 1849 to allow east–west through traffic, costing £650,000 and three lives when part of the viaduct at Oxford road collapsed January 1849. With the opening of the 'extension' to Altrincham, a new, elevated station was opened at Oxford Road where Altrincham trains terminated.

Above: Deansgate aka Knott Mill Station, built by the MSJ&A in 1896 replacing an earlier timber structure of 1849 described as being an eyesore. (Author)

Left: Some of the old railway remains: MSJ&A monogram still proudly displayed at Knott Mill. (Author)

Rail, road and canal unite at the junction of Deansgate and Whitworth Street, the beautiful iron bridges built by the MSJ&A in 1849 still doing what they were designed for. (Author)

What it did not provide was easy access from Victoria to London Road (or vice versa) without a reversal at Ordsall Lane; something partially corrected by the 'Windsor Link' in 1988. The 2016 Ordsall Chord, however, will provide direct through running from Victoria to Piccadilly (née London Road), but at the loss of the main line connection at Liverpool Road Station, Manchester's first – and the world's oldest – passenger railway station.

To overcome the lack of through-running from London Road to Victoria, the M&B proposed building a link from London Road to Victoria, tunnelling under part of the eastern side of the city. This elaborate proposal, however, came to naught due to the engineering difficulties and differences in elevation between the two stations of some 16 feet, which would have precluded through-running. Once again, the idea did not lay dormant for long; the newly formed Lancashire & Yorkshire Railway constructed a curving, steeply graded branch line from Midland Junction near Ardwick through to Miles Platting to allow freight working between the two stations. This 1-mile-1,561-yard-long, single-track branch was opened in November 1848, forming an important link from Birmingham and the Potteries to Leeds and thence Hull. Passenger working over it began in 1852; it was doubled in 1865, only to be closed ninety-nine years later.

In order to reach this point of maturity, the in-fighting and rivalry between these companies had to be laid to rest. As we have seen, the beleaguered M&B struggled for survival against the GJR – even to the point of abandoning its proposed extension to

Remains of the Ardwick–Miles Platting branch built by the Manchester & Leeds Railway to join London Road with Victoria. (Author)

Rugby in order to secure running rights to Birmingham. The M&B should have been a natural ally of the London & Birmingham, but they too were opposed to the M&B extension through the Potteries and the Trent Valley to Rugby, which would have taken a considerable portion of their traffic. It was only in 1846 that Sir Robert Peel was able to cut the first sod of the Trent Valley Line, but on the proviso that when completed it be sold to the London & Birmingham; by which point the M&B had amalgamated with the London concern. This amalgamation in September 1845 was a tactical move by the M&B to challenge the Midland Railway's inroads into the North West – it 'put the extinguisher on ambitious competitors'. The London & Birmingham now had a route between London and Manchester, wholly owned and operated by a single company that was some fifteen miles shorter than the rival route via the GJR: 84 miles compared to 99. Journey time to Birmingham was four hours, and London nine and a half, including a half-hour interval at Birmingham for refreshments.

On its part, the GJR had absorbed the L&M in order to consolidate its position further, absorbed the Bolton & Leigh and Leigh & Kenyon Railways, and established control of the North Union Railway; running from Parkside Junction on the L&M up to Preston. This absorption placed the GJR in a much stronger position in the north and allowed it to be able to withstand attacks from its main rival, the London & Birmingham. Amalgamation of the M&B with the L&B, however, left the GJR in a somewhat isolated position, and following the retirement of John Moss – he was also Chair of the L&M – in October 1845, a more cordial relationship began with its former rival; nothing less than an 'astonishing change in GJR tactics', leading to the GJR Board seeking amalgamation and consolidation with the L&B. This more cordial relationship was not only prompted by the retirement of key personalities, but by a major external threat – the Great Western was threatening to build a line to Birmingham, with the very real spectre of Brunel's broad gauge heading even further north. Now that the L&B had a more direct, and indeed shorter, route to Manchester, the GJR found itself possibly being denied access to London. Mark Huish, general manager of the GJR, used the possibility of the Broad Gauge reaching Birmingham to make overtures with the GWR and investigate the cost of adding an extra rail to the GJR and L&M, concluding that such conversion to the broad gauge could be made at a reasonable cost. With this threat, Charles Lawrence – the new Chair of the GJR – entered into more constructive dialogue with the L&B, and amalgamation was 'almost immediately decided upon' in spring 1846. From 1 January 1845 the L&B and the GJR were already working together 'as one system' as a prelude to formal amalgamation on 16 July 1846 to form the London & North Western Railway. Upon formation, therefore, the LNWR had a route from London Euston via Birmingham to Manchester, and as far north as Preston and thence Lancaster. Calling itself the 'Premier Line', and 'the oldest in the business', the LNWR was Britain's largest joint-stock company.

Where it all began in 1830: Liverpool Road, Manchester. (Author)

But what of the LNWR's transpennine rivals? The M&L was busy extending its influence west into Lancashire and consolidating its position as the major transpennine route into Yorkshire. It was decided at a company meeting in December 1846 to change the name of the company to one 'more expressive of the extent and importance ... of the system'. The name chosen was the Lancashire & Yorkshire Railway, confirmed by an Act of 9 July 1847, by which the L&Y also absorbed the Wakefield, Pontefract & Goole and the Ashton, Stalybridge & Liverpool Junction Railways. The MB&B had been absorbed during the previous year. The L&Y became one of Britain's major railway companies. Even though it had a route mileage of only around 600 miles, the intensity of its operations – running as it did through the densely populated industrial north – is shown by it owning 1,650 locomotives by 1900. Twenty-two years later, the L&Y amalgamated with the LNWR.

Thus, in just twenty years after the opening of the Liverpool & Manchester Railway, Manchester could boast three mainline passenger stations (London Road, Victoria, New Bailey Street) and two goods station (Liverpool Road, Oldham Road), providing rail services to Liverpool, Preston, Leeds, Hull, Birmingham and London.